c/2

C0-APG-136

THE NEW DEAL IN ACTION

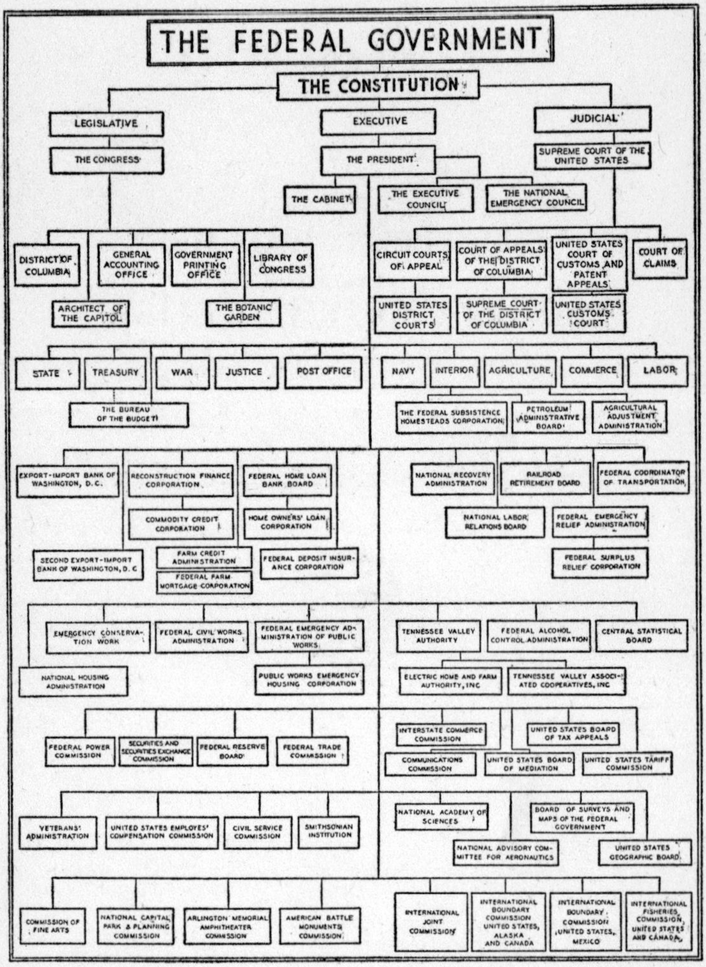
THE FEDERAL GOVERNMENT
THE CONSTITUTION
LEGISLATIVE
EXECUTIVE
JUDICIAL
THE CONGRESS
THE PRESIDENT
SUPREME COURT OF THE UNITED STATES
THE CABINET
THE EXECUTIVE COUNCIL
THE NATIONAL EMERGENCY COUNCIL
DISTRICT OF COLUMBIA
GENERAL ACCOUNTING OFFICE
GOVERNMENT PRINTING OFFICE
LIBRARY OF CONGRESS
ARCHITECT OF THE CAPITOL
THE BOTANIC GARDEN
CIRCUIT COURTS OF APPEAL
COURT OF APPEALS OF THE DISTRICT OF COLUMBIA
UNITED STATES COURT OF CUSTOMS AND PATENT APPEALS
COURT OF CLAIMS
UNITED STATES DISTRICT COURTS
SUPREME COURT OF THE DISTRICT OF COLUMBIA
UNITED STATES CUSTOMS COURT
STATE
TREASURY
WAR
JUSTICE
POST OFFICE
NAVY
INTERIOR
AGRICULTURE
COMMERCE
LABOR
THE BUREAU OF THE BUDGET
THE FEDERAL SUBSISTENCE HOMESTEADS CORPORATION
PETROLEUM ADMINISTRATIVE BOARD
AGRICULTURAL ADJUSTMENT ADMINISTRATION
EXPORT-IMPORT BANK OF WASHINGTON, D. C.
RECONSTRUCTION FINANCE CORPORATION
FEDERAL HOME LOAN BANK BOARD
COMMODITY CREDIT CORPORATION
HOME OWNERS' LOAN CORPORATION
SECOND EXPORT-IMPORT BANK OF WASHINGTON, D. C
FARM CREDIT ADMINISTRATION
FEDERAL FARM MORTGAGE CORPORATION
FEDERAL DEPOSIT INSURANCE CORPORATION
NATIONAL RECOVERY ADMINISTRATION
RAILROAD RETIREMENT BOARD
FEDERAL COORDINATOR OF TRANSPORTATION
NATIONAL LABOR RELATIONS BOARD
FEDERAL EMERGENCY RELIEF ADMINISTRATION
FEDERAL SURPLUS RELIEF CORPORATION
EMERGENCY CONSERVATION WORK
FEDERAL CIVIL WORKS ADMINISTRATION
FEDERAL EMERGENCY ADMINISTRATION OF PUBLIC WORKS
NATIONAL HOUSING ADMINISTRATION
PUBLIC WORKS EMERGENCY HOUSING CORPORATION
TENNESSEE VALLEY AUTHORITY
FEDERAL ALCOHOL CONTROL ADMINISTRATION
CENTRAL STATISTICAL BOARD
ELECTRIC HOME AND FARM AUTHORITY, INC
TENNESSEE VALLEY ASSOCIATED COOPERATIVES, INC
FEDERAL POWER COMMISSION
SECURITIES AND SECURITIES EXCHANGE COMMISSION
FEDERAL RESERVE BOARD
FEDERAL TRADE COMMISSION
INTERSTATE COMMERCE COMMISSION
UNITED STATES BOARD OF TAX APPEALS
COMMUNICATIONS COMMISSION
UNITED STATES BOARD OF MEDIATION
UNITED STATES TARIFF COMMISSION
VETERANS' ADMINISTRATION
UNITED STATES EMPLOYES' COMPENSATION COMMISSION
CIVIL SERVICE COMMISSION
SMITHSONIAN INSTITUTION
NATIONAL ACADEMY OF SCIENCES
BOARD OF SURVEYS AND MAPS OF THE FEDERAL GOVERNMENT
NATIONAL ADVISORY COMMITTEE FOR AERONAUTICS
UNITED STATES GEOGRAPHIC BOARD
COMMISSION OF FINE ARTS
NATIONAL CAPITAL PARK & PLANNING COMMISSION
ARLINGTON MEMORIAL AMPHITHEATER COMMISSION
AMERICAN BATTLE MONUMENTS COMMISSION
INTERNATIONAL JOINT COMMISSION
INTERNATIONAL BOUNDARY COMMISSION UNITED STATES, ALASKA AND CANADA
INTERNATIONAL BOUNDARY COMMISSION UNITED STATES, MEXICO
INTERNATIONAL FISHERIES COMMISSION, UNITED STATES AND CANADA

WITHDRAWN

The New Deal in Action

BY

SCHUYLER C. WALLACE

DEPARTMENT OF PUBLIC LAW
COLUMBIA UNIVERSITY

HARPER & BROTHERS PUBLISHERS
NEW YORK AND LONDON

THE NEW DEAL IN ACTION
Copyright, 1934, by Harper & Brothers
Printed in the United States of America
FOURTH EDITION
B-K

*All rights in this book are reserved
No part of the text may be reproduced in any manner whatsoever without written permission. For information address
Harper & Brothers.*

HC
106
.3
.W324

To

E. G. W.

MAR 28 1935

46845

PREFACE

In the pages which follow I have been attempting merely a description of the activities of the Roosevelt Administration in its endeavor to stay the course of the depression, to prevent the proletarianization of large sections of the middle class and to introduce into our economy corrections designed to restore that balance of interests fundamental to the proper functioning of our economic order. And to analyse the reasoning upon which these efforts are based.

Unlike the devotees of either classical or Marxian economics I find it impossible to come to any very definite conclusions as to the future. To me the imponderables of both politics and economics are of such tremendous importance that any attempt to prognosticate the future by logical deduction from the premises of either the classical or Marxian economists is as futile as the logical exercises of the schoolmen. It is for this reason that I am forced to come again and again to the exceedingly unsatisfactory conclusion—only time will tell.

Despite this limitation I hope that this attempt to describe what has been going on in Washington and to explain the reasoning which has underlain the actions taken may, nevertheless, be of service.

Much of the material contained in these pages has previously appeared in the magazine *Today* in somewhat different form. Indeed the reaction to the articles which have been published in *Today* is my chief justification for presenting the material in book form.

—Schuyler C. Wallace.

Columbia University
New York City

TABLE OF CONTENTS

INTRODUCTION

FINANCE

AGRICULTURE

INDUSTRY

INTRODUCTION

CHAPTER ONE

CATACLYSM

"THEN came the crash. . . . Plants became idle. Men lost their jobs, purchasing power dried up, banks became frightened and started calling loans. Those who had money were afraid to part with it. Credit declined, and unemployment mounted."[1] In these words Franklin D. Roosevelt in July, 1932, described the events of the two years immediately preceding. And such was the momentum of the downward spiral of our economic order that by Inauguration Day fourteen million persons were out of work. Every bank in the country had closed. Our financial system had collapsed.

What was the explanation of the cataclysm?

In the course of the campaign of 1932 the Democratic nominee presented to the country his analysis of the factors responsible for the débâcle. An analysis which might be summed up in the single word—maladjustment.

It was the New York Governor's opinion that various segments of the national economy had gotten so critically out of alignment that a national if not a world catastrophe was inevitable. As he saw it an industrial system such as that which had developed in the United States could function smoothly only if its various segments were kept in proper economic balance, with "a real community of interest—not only among the sections of this great coun-

[1] Franklin D. Roosevelt, *Looking Forward*, p. 28.

try, but among the economic units and the various groups in these units."

Such a balance of interests had not in fact been maintained. A cataclysm was, in consequence, inevitable.

Most fundamental of the maladjustments in our national economy, as Mr. Roosevelt visualized it, were: first, the tremendous discrepancy which had grown up between agriculture and industry; second, the disproportionate distribution of income between the consuming and investing classes; and third, lack of organization in industry itself which made industrial planning exceedingly difficult, if not altogether impossible. Contributory to these major maladjustments was a series of lesser ones, not least among which was a mistaken tariff policy, an unwise policy of foreign loans, and an uncontrolled credit system. Less important, perhaps, but nevertheless significant, were still other maladjustments which had developed in the field of transportation, in connection with the public utilities, and in the organization of the government itself.

The fact that 22 per cent of the population deriving its income from agriculture received only 7 per cent of the national income was, to Mr. Roosevelt, conclusive evidence of a tremendous disproportion in the relation of agriculture to the rest of our national economy. In 1920, this same segment of the population had received 15 per cent of the national income. This 8-per-cent drop in income, it seemed evident to the Democratic nominee, was one of the most significant factors contributing to the débâcle, disastrous to agriculture and industry alike. For as he saw it, the drying up of purchasing power in this vast segment of the population could have but one result, the cessation of that percentage of city industry which had theretofore been supplying the demands of this part of the national community.

Outstanding among the numerous subsidiary causes of this development was an unquestionably iniquitous tariff policy—a policy which "destroyed the foreign markets for our exportable surplus," which violated all principles of international trade and forced "the retaliation of the other nations of the world"; a policy which at the same time contributed to a steady increase in the domestic price of industrial products. The outcome was catastrophic so far as agriculture was concerned since "the principal cash crops of our farms are produced much in excess of our requirements." They must, in consequence, be sold in the world markets at the world price. However, since in many of our industries this is not the case, the American farmer was faced with the necessity of selling on a free-trade basis, and purchasing on a protected one.

The farmer's plight, moreover, was accentuated by improvident loans to agricultural countries. Notwithstanding the fact that these loans were used by the recipients for industrial rather than agricultural purposes, the only way the loans could be repaid was through the sale of ever-increasing agricultural surpluses. These loans, therefore, stimulated our debtors to increase their agricutural production to a maximum. As a result international sales rivalry in agricultural surpluses became increasingly severe, while prices for agricultural commodities dropped still further.

Equally important in Mr. Roosevelt's eyes was the maladjustment in the distribution of income between the consuming and investing classes, generally. In the decade preceding 1929 he believed we "had completed a vast cycle of building" ostensibly for the purpose of reconstruction following the ravages of war, but actually we had gone far beyond that, in fact "far beyond our national and normal needs.

"During that time the cold figures of finance prove that there was little or no drop in the prices the consumer had to pay, although those same figures prove that the cost of production fell very greatly; corporate profits resulting from this period were enormous; at the same time little of the profit was devoted to the reduction of prices. The consumer was forgotten. Little went into increased wages; the worker was forgotten, and by no means an adequate proportion was paid out in dividends—the stockholder was forgotten. Incidentally, very little was taken in taxation by the beneficent government of those days. What was the result? Enormous corporate surpluses piled up—the most stupendous in history. These surpluses went chiefly in two directions: first, into new and unnecessary plants which now stand stark and idle; second, into the call-money market of Wall Street, either directly by the corporations or indirectly through the banks." [2]

Equally clear to the Democratic nominee were the consequences of an unplanned economy. He felt it impossible to review "the history of our industrial advance without being struck by its haphazardness, with the gigantic waste with which it [has] been accomplished and with the superfluous duplication of productive facilities, the continuous scrapping of still useful equipment, the tremendous mortality in industrial and commercial undertakings, the thousands of dead-end trails into which enterprise has been lured, the profligate waste of natural resources." Much of this waste, he believed, was the

[2] Franklin D. Roosevelt, *Looking Forward,* p. 28.

inevitable by-product of progress in society. But much of it, he was convinced, "could have been prevented by greater foresight and by a larger measure of social planning. . . ."

Herein Mr. Roosevelt perceived the great challenge of the future.

A mistaken tariff policy, in addition to being one of the contributory causes to the agricultural depression, was, in his eyes, a large contributory factor in the débâcle in industry also. Deprived of the American market, the other nations of the world sought to maintain an outlet for their surpluses through mutual trade agreements, import quotas, tariffs and all the other technicalities which the ingenuity of their statesmen could devise. "The ink on the Grundy bill was hardly dry before the foreign markets commenced their program of retaliation. Brick against brick, they built their walls against us."

What was the result? Within the two years which followed the passage of the Grundy tariff, our foreign trade declined fully 50 per cent. In June, 1930, the month of the passage of the Grundy bill, our exports were valued at $394,000,000, our imports at $250,000,000. In June, 1932, our exports were worth $115,000,000; our imports worth, $78,000,000. During these same two years American manufacturers established 258 factories in foreign countries as the only practical method of penetrating the newly established tariff barriers.

Equally ill-advised, thought Mr. Roosevelt, was our policy of foreign loans. For a time we practically financed not only our entire export trade, but the repayment of previously accumulated debts, both principal and interest. The temporary effect of our financial policy was an artificial stimulus of our foreign trade and, in consequence, of our entire industrial system. The final result was inevitable. "When we began to diminish the financing in 1929 the economic structure of the world began to totter. When in 1930 we imposed the Grundy tariff, the tottering structure collapsed."

No less significant from Mr. Roosevelt's point of view were the consequences of "new era" banking, which permitted the utilization of the tremendous banking resources of the country for the purpose of stock speculation. This situation developed partly as a result of the psychology of the era and partly because many banking institutions had become nothing more or less than adjuncts to glorified brokerage houses and securities firms. The cards were stacked for the stock-market speculation which eventuated, but just as inevitable was it that collapse would ensue.

Certain practices which had developed in the utility field contributed their share both to the financial débâcle and to the maladjustment in the distribution of income between consumers and investors. Certain of the utility magnates at least appear to have been little troubled by scruples either in their manipulation of the financial structure of their enterprises or in the charges they made to the consumer. Their financial activities were in many cases actually fraudulent; in others, anti-social. Whether the maintenance of a sales price at fifteen times the actual cost of production was any less anti-social seems exceedingly dubious.

The maladjustment in the field of transportation was of a somewhat different character. As Mr. Roosevelt saw it, the railroads were being forced to meet a competition fundamentally unfair in character. Not only were busses and trucks carrying passengers and commodities over a publicly built and publicly maintained right of way, but they were subjected to little or no regulation as to wages, hours of labor, or services rendered. The railroads were on the contrary, not only subject to stringent regulation in these particulars, but in many cases they were compelled to compete with each other quite unreasonably.

Of a different character was the maladjustment which had developed within the government itself. The cost of the governmental machine which had been built up in the era of prosperity was simply too great to be maintained in the day of adversity. The budget had to be balanced. Governmental reorganization, national, state, and local, had become imperative. Although Mr. Roosevelt did not contend that the maladjustment in government had been one of the fundamental causes of the depression, he did insist that it seriously impaired the possibility of recovery.

These, then, were the causes of the depression as Mr. Roosevelt saw them, and this the picture of the world which was in his mind when on March 4, 1933, he was sworn in as President of the United States.

CHAPTER TWO

RECONSTRUCTION

ACTION was the order of the day. Rightly or wrongly, something had to be done. A concerted attack upon the causes of the depression was imperative. Such was the psychology of the American people on March 4, 1933.

Hardly had the administration taken office when the attack began. The banking crisis made it necessary that the first action be taken in the field of finance. A national bank holiday was proclaimed. Emergency legislation was rushed through. The rules of the Federal Reserve System relative to the issuance of currency were liberalized. State banks were permitted to secure federal assistance. The slow-moving machinery of receiverships was superseded by the more rapidly moving administrative device of conservatorships. Foreign exchange operations were put under the control of the Federal Reserve Bank and closed banks were allowed to reopen only as they were found to be sound. So effective were the measures taken by the administration that within three weeks the Federal Reserve Bank notes outstanding had declined $185,000,000. The banking crisis was over. From the point of view of the administration, however, the temporary solution of the banking crisis did not constitute a correction of the fundamental defects of our financial system. Much remained to be done.

On March 10th, the President issued an order forbidding the export of gold except upon license by the Treasury. April 5th there came the order prohibiting hoarding, followed on April 20th by another prohibiting the export of gold. We had gone off the gold standard.

If the American people had voted for action, they were certainly getting it.

May 12th, the so-called Thomas Amendment passed. By this enactment there were concentrated in the President's hands tremendous powers which might or might not be used for inflation. By joint resolution on June 5th, the two Houses of Congress declared null and void the gold clause of any contract, public or private, subject to the jurisdiction of the United States.

The currency question temporarily settled, the banking maladjustments remained to be considered. On June 16th the Glass-Steagall bill was passed. The relation of all Federal Reserve Banks to their security affiliates was sharply scrutinized, and divorce proceedings instituted. Branch banking was to be permitted in any state extending the privilege to its state institutions. The Federal Reserve Board was empowered to deny its credit facilities to any bank unduly encouraging speculation, and no member bank was any longer to be permitted to place call loans "for others."

Executive officers were prohibited from borrowing from their own banks and were required to report all loans secured from others. Membership in the Federal Reserve System was greatly widened, and a deposit guarantee feature was added.

Thus was the attack on many of the maladjustments in the banking field consummated.

As a further remedial measure a Securities Act was passed. According to the provisions of this Act not only were specific data required as to the financial status of the companies issuing new securities, but a misstatement of fact was to be accepted as a basis for suit against companies and underwriters alike.

There remained the tremendous task of balancing the budget. Drastic economies were made in the ordinary running expenses of the government; salaries were cut, positions were eliminated, pensions drastically reduced, and new sources of revenue provided. An extraordinary budget was enacted to take care of emergency expenditures, to be financed largely through the issuance of bonds. Still further taxes were added in an endeavor to cover both the carrying charges and the sums necessary for an amortization of the principal.

While this attack upon maladjustments in the field of finance was being launched, another was being prepared in the realm of agriculture. Two lines of assault were projected—refinancing and the raising of agricultural price levels. To accomplish the first of these purposes, the Farm Loan Act was amended and a Farm Credit Act passed. Through the machinery thus set up the attempt was to be made to refinance farm mortgages and extend farm loans on a scale never before known in American history.

Through the Agricultural Adjustment Act an attempt was to be made to increase agricultural prices by limiting production. This was to be accomplished either by renting land from the farmers directly, or paying the farmers a subsidy if they restricted their production in accordance with the government's stipulations. The money for this was to come from processing taxes levied on agricultural commodities. "The bounty to the cotton-growers was to come from a tax levied on the making of cotton goods;

the payment to the wheat-growers from a tax on the conversion of wheat into flour."

Through these measures it was hoped that the maladjustment between agriculture and industry might be rectified and that the farming community might thus come closer to receiving a more proportionate share of the national income.

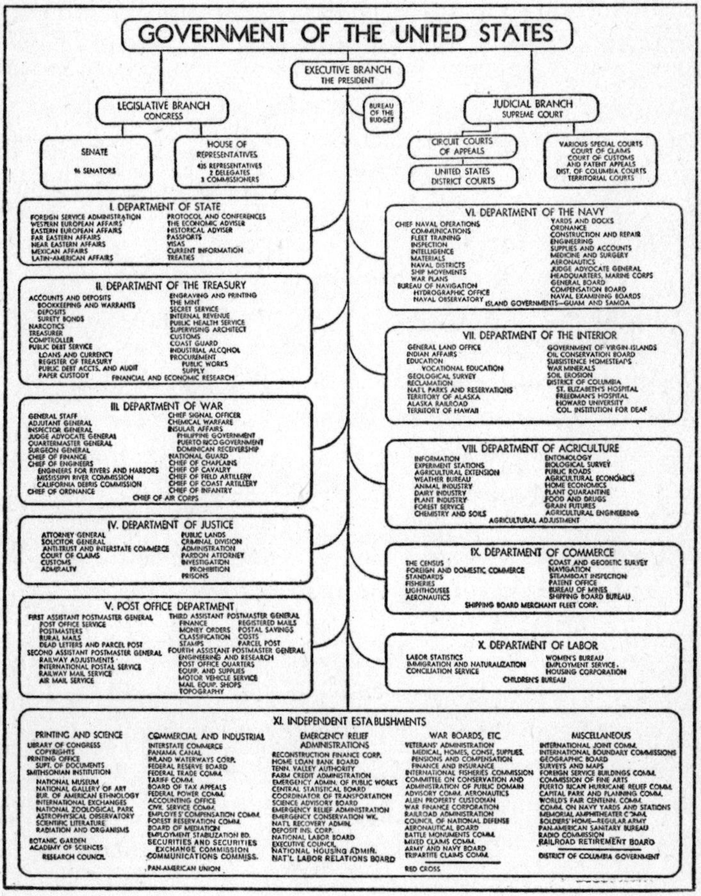

Within industry itself there were numerous maladjustments, most fundamental of which was the fact that between thirteen and fourteen million men were out of work. Action was imperative. The National Industrial Recovery Act was drafted and enacted. Under it, private industry was given the opportunity to undertake "effective economic coordination" unhampered by the restrictions of anti-trust laws.

Hours were to be shortened, child labor was to be eliminated, and a minimum wage for the workers in each industry established. Thus the beginnings at least of a planned economy were made possible, and the most sinister aspects of *laissez-faire* competition, undesirably long hours, child labor and sweat-shop wages, were eliminated, while an increase in employment was provided.

In a somewhat different category, but nevertheless exceedingly important in this major offensive against fundamental maladjustments in industry, were the Railroad Relief Act and the Utility Acts. The first of these provided for a coordinator of Transportation, whose function was to require such action on the part of the carriers as would avoid an unnecessary duplication of services and facilities, permit the joint use of terminals and trackage, and compel such other action as would promote the most efficient operation of our railroad system. The bill incidentally brought under federal regulation the holding companies, which Mr. Roosevelt had described in the course of the campaign as "financial comets that have been roving through the system, spending other people's money in financial gambling through which a lot of money has been lost and a good deal of damage done." In like manner, the Tennessee Valley Authority was set up, designed not only to develop the tremendous territory centering around Muscle Shoals, but also to act as a yardstick against which the efficiency of private utilities might be measured.

Two tasks remained. The pump had yet to be primed. Relief was still to be provided.

True, some water had been poured down the pump through the Federal Farm Credit Act, and the Emergency Transportation Act. But this was not enough. Millions upon millions of dollars still remained frozen. The Home Loan Act was passed, making available to the small-home-owner $2,200,000,000, and further loans to railroads, insurance companies, and various financial institutions were made possible.

Much more important, a huge public works program was authorized. A Public Works Administration was created. Three billion three hundred million dollars all told could be expended under its authority. All contracts let in connection with the expenditure of this money must specify a thirty-hour week for labor, reasonable wages, and a maximum of human labor to be used in lieu of machinery.

An Unemployment Relief Bill was passed, establishing the Civilian Conservation Corps. A Federal Relief Administration was established to effect a closer cooperation between Federal and state relief projects, and to make to the states outright gifts to aggregate not over $250,000,000. These were essentially temporary relief measures. More significant, perhaps, was the act creating the United States Unemployment Service.

These constituted the principal enactments under the New Deal. This was the Rooseveltian attack upon the depression. Underlying them all was the Rooseveltian philosophy of a concert of interests. Taken together, they represented an attempt to stay the course of the deflation, to prevent the proletarianization of large sections of the middle class and to introduce into our national economy corrections designed to restore that balance of interests fundamental to the proper functioning of our economic order.

FINANCE

CHAPTER THREE

THE BANKING DÉBÂCLE

ON MARCH 4, 1933, every bank in the United States had closed its doors. This was undoubtedly the most spectacular episode of the whole depression.

Among the various factors which contributed to the collapse, four stand out above all others—the post-war inflation, certain basic defects in the structure and management of our banks, the European financial hurricane, and the hoarding panic.[1]

The fundamental cause of the cataclysm was in all probability the post-war inflation. In 1919 the bank loans outstanding totalled $24,923,000,000; in 1929 the total was $41,531,000,000. In other words our banking system had, in the ten years before the crash, almost doubled the amount of credit outstanding. This credit was used for varied purposes. In part it went into the tremendous land speculations in Florida and elsewhere; in part, it went into the stock-market orgy; in part, it went to Europe in the form of loans; in part, it was used for installment buying. The catalog is incomplete. One fact, however, is clear. There occurred during this decade the most tremendous peace-time inflation the United States has ever witnessed. That inflation, weakening as it did the credit structure of the entire nation, was to constitute the stage upon which the drama of 1929 was to be enacted.

[1] This analysis is drawn largely from *The Banking Crisis*, by Jules I. Bogan and Marcus Nadler.

Similarly contributory to the collapse of the American banking system were certain basic defects of management and structure. Unlike most banking systems, that of the United States was and is broken up into numerous units, which numbered at one time thirty thousand. Owing to the fact that the banking laws of many states permit the organization of banks with totally inadequate capital resources; owing also, perhaps, to the fact that the smaller institutions found it difficult, if not impossible, to secure that diversification of business requisite for safety, many of the smaller units in the banking system have been at all times exceedingly weak, if not actually insolvent.

It was, therefore, not surprising to students of banking that when the agricultural depression hit the country in 1921, many of these smaller institutions went to the wall. Indeed, the history of banking in the United States from 1921 to 1929 is a history of bank failures ranging from a low of 354 in 1922 to a high of 956 in 1926.

Bank failures, unfortunately, are not isolated phenomena. The failure of one bank quite frequently starts a run on another. Thus the history of bank failures from 1921 to 1929 is without question the history of the slow impairment of public confidence in all banking institutions in large sections of the country.

No less important in contributing to the débâcle were certain fundamental defects of management. Most significant among these was not the fact that under the laws of many states the butcher, the baker, and candlestick-maker, with little or no experience in finance, could organize a banking institution, but rather a fundamental shift in banking policy which affected almost the entire banking fraternity—the shift from commercial to investment banking.

Down to the beginning of the twentieth century most of the commercial banks throughout the country were engaged primarily in commercial banking. The largest portion of their investments were in short-time self-liquidating commercial paper. Consequently, when the Bank of Squedunk loaned Farmer Brown the money with which to hire cherry-pickers, the officers of the bank did so with the full knowledge that a cherry crop existed, that the crop would be picked, shipped, and marketed, and that, unless an act of God intervened, by the end of sixty days Farmer Brown would receive from the sale of his cherries a sum five or six times the amount the bank loaned him. They knew, therefore, that their loan was sound, and, equally important, that it would be liquidated very shortly. Thus the officers of the bank might well feel that the bank was in a position to meet practically any demand which its depositors might make upon it.

With the turn of the twentieth century and the rise of the modern corporation with enormous corporate surpluses the demand for this type of transaction diminished. In consequence, the profits from this type of transaction diminished likewise. In a desperate endeavor to retain their previous profits, the commercial banks turned more and more to the investment banking business, lending, on long-term investments, money which had been deposited with them, subject to withdrawal upon demand.

These long-term investments were for the most part loans on mortgages or securities.

Since most mortgages have a fixed term for which they run, it is obvious that the money so invested could no longer be considered fluid. In the event of a run the funds invested in this type of security were simply frozen.

In normal times loans on stocks and bonds, on the contrary, preserve at least the appearance of liquidity, for it is then possible for an individual institution to dump these securities on the market, if forced to do so, and thus retrieve its loans. As a matter of fact, however, these loans were not and are not liquid, in the same sense loans secured by short-term, self-liquidating paper may be said to be. Instead they are, or shortly become, a significant part of the long-term investment funds of the country. The course of events which has followed the stock-market crash of 1929 has made this point much clearer than it could possibly be made by any hypothetical illustration.

When, after the crash of 1929, it became necessary for individual banks to liquidate their loans, security after security was dumped on the market. The net result was a decline in values at such a rate that an increasing number of institutions found it absolutely impossible to collect through the sale of collateral the amount of the loans outstanding. And had the banking panic been allowed to run its course without governmental interference, the impossibility of suddenly withdrawing the short-term funds from the long-term investment market would have been even more clearly revealed. Values would have been driven down to practically nothing. Thus, although in normal times, loans on stocks and bonds may preserve the appearance of liquidity, the experience of the last several years has conclusively proven that such appearances are indeed deceptive. Thus, it is easily seen, in retrospect, that the American banking system in a semi-frozen condition at this time faced a financial crisis demanding the utmost liquidity.

It was in Europe, rather than in the United States, however, that the financial storm first broke. The Kredit Anstalt, one of the largest and most respected banking institutions in Austria, a banking institution which, by virtue of its Rothschild connection, had a prestige far beyond the boundaries of Austria, got into difficulties. The fact that this one bank controlled approximately two-thirds of the industrial production of Austria was in itself significant. More significant, however, was the fact that its tremendous reputation had enabled it to borrow "relatively large amounts of short-term funds abroad." Once the news got out that the Kredit Anstalt was in difficulties, panic swept Vienna. A huge run followed. Foreign capital took alarm and proceeded to withdraw its deposits. So serious had the situation become that it shortly became evident that the Austrian government, unaided, would be unable to save the situation. An attempt was made to borrow money abroad.

France used the opportunity to bring pressure to bear upon Austria to renounce "the Customs Union with Germany as the price of its participation in the loan." Austria refused. The Bank of England, either because of the fact that English bankers already had tremendous sums invested in Central Europe or because the officials of the bank recognized the seriousness of the situation which was impending, carried the loan alone.

This action aroused both the ire and the fear of the French—ire because Great Britain had prevented France from accomplishing her political objective; fear because it was shortly to become evident that the British loan in and of itself would not be sufficient to save the Kredit Anstalt and that English financiers, in consequence, were on the point of suffering tremendous losses in Central Europe. French investors, with balances in England, seriously considered the question of withdrawing their deposits. Some of them actually did so.

As the French had foreseen, the British loan was not sufficient to save the Austrian institution. The Kredit Anstalt collapsed.

We in the United States, with no close ties with Europe, find it difficult to understand why the collapse of the Kredit Anstalt should have started a run on the banks of Central Europe generally. Perhaps if we should try to imagine the consequences which would follow in the United States if the entire Chicago banking system were to collapse we might obtain a commensurate picture. The collapse of the famous Rothschild institution raised a question everywhere throughout Central Europe as to the soundness of their banking institutions. The run in Germany very shortly became serious. Not only did foreign financiers withdraw the balances they had in German banks, but Germans themselves, fearing for the safety of their domestic banking institutions, transferred enormous sums to Switzerland, Holland, and elsewhere. It is estimated that during the first seven months of 1931 this "flight of capital deprived Germany of approximately 3,500,000,000 marks."

The Reichsbank likewise appealed for foreign aid, and on June 25, 1931, received a short-term grant of credit totaling $100,000,000 from the Bank for International Settlements, the Bank of England, the Bank of France, and the Federal Reserve Bank of New York. The flight from the mark, nevertheless, continued. It shortly became evident that with this money being withdrawn by Germans and foreigners alike from German banks and with the German government faced with the necessity of withdrawing still more money from its banks for reparation payments, the German banking system would follow that of Austria into total collapse.

It was at this juncture of affairs that Mr. Hoover proposed a moratorium on both reparations and war debts. The gesture was magnificent and might have staved off the collapse. Unfortunately, however, Mr. Hoover had bungled his diplomacy. Once again France, for both political and financial reasons, hesitated, and by the time the technicalities upon which the French insisted had been worked out the psychological effect of the gesture upon Germany was lost. The run continued. The German banking system collapsed.

The Bank of England now had a tremendous sum of money frozen by virtue of the collapse of the Kredit Anstalt and a second tremendous sum through the collapse of the German banking system. Single-handed it had thwarted France's political desires in connection with Austria, and, together with the United States, had put such pressure on France in connection with the moratorium that the French were both politically alienated and financially apprehensive. Equally important was the fact that certain British financiers had individually lost tremendous sums in the collapse of both the Austrian and German banking systems. In consequence the French, already alarmed as to the soundness of the British financial institutions, began post haste to withdraw their balances, at the time estimated to amount to almost $300,000,000.[2] A general run on the London money market followed. Like the Germans and the Austrians, the English attempted to support their currency by heavy borrowings from abroad. Unfortunately, the run, once started, accumulated such momentum that, despite the

[2] The Bank of France, be it said, did not withdraw a single cent from the London money market during the entire panic and lost in consequence a sum equal to its entire capital.

action of the government, it became dubious as to whether the Bank of England could stand the strain and remain on the gold standard. Further foreign assistance was not forthcoming and, sooner than lose her total gold reserve, England went off the gold standard. The collapse of the pound inevitably took most of the British Dominions and colonies and the Scandinavian countries down with it.

France and the United States alone, therefore, remained unshaken by the financial hurricane which was sweeping across the world.

Nevertheless, the stage was set for the American débâcle.

The downward spiral of the agricultural depression from 1921 to 1929 had resulted in the bank failures already referred to. The collapse of between five and six thousand banks during this era could produce no other result in the areas affected, than the impairment of the confidence of the people, in the soundness of all banking institutions.

The collapse of the stock market and the industrial depression which followed did nothing, needless to say, to restore that shattered confidence. The number of bank failures increased, 1,345 banks closing their doors in 1930, 2,298 in 1931, and 1,456 in 1932.

Thus, at the very time the financial storm was sweeping over England, clouds were gathering in the United States. Although the failure of the Bank of United States, December 15, 1930, may be said to mark the beginning of the hoarding panic which was to close every bank in the United States, the first run on the American dollar did not begin until the fall of 1931, when, in a space of two months, the United States lost $700,000,000 in gold. This run was in part the natural outcome of the monetary disturbances in Europe and in part a revelation of a feeling of uneasiness on the part of Europe relative to our banking institutions. The Federal Reserve banks met this run dollar for dollar. In consequence, the run subsided and early in November money began to flow back to the United States. The continuance of bank failures, however, caused largely by the downward sweep of the business cycle, the previous bad management of our American banking institutions, and the unit system of banking, further undermined the morale of the public.

At the suggestion of the Hoover administration, the National Credit Corporation was formed for the purpose of relieving, if possible, the pressure upon the weaker banks. The National Credit Corporation was succeeded, on January 22, 1932, by the Reconstruction Finance Corporation, similarly designed to alleviate this pressure by the lending of government money to weak institutions. Foreign capital, regarding such action on the part of the administration to be an admission of weakness, took flight again. Caught by the contagion, a number of Americans began to withdraw their deposits from American banks and invest them abroad. The crash of Kreuger and Toll carried down with it one exceeding reputable investment banking house and still further undermined the confidence of the public at home and abroad.

The depression, one might remark, parenthetically, was rushing on.

In order further to alleviate the pressure on the banks and to stop, if possible, the progress of the depression, the Federal Reserve Board embarked on an easy-money policy. Throughout the Middle West the demand for inflation almost daily grew stronger. The Goldsboro bill, an inflationary measure, actually passed the House of

Representatives. In the meantime no effective steps had been taken to balance the budget. Would not the United States, like England, be driven off the gold standard? Frightened at the prospect, foreign capital again took flight and within two months approximately $250,000,000 in gold had again been withdrawn.

As a matter of fact, had this been the only strain to which the American banking system had been subjected we could and would have stood up under it without any question. All Europe combined could not have driven us off the gold standard. Unfortunately, the European run, combined with continuing banking failures at home, caused a great uneasiness on the part of the American public. Hoarding not only continued, but increased in volume. This in itself intensified the difficulties of the banks. Securities had to be dumped on the market, thus accelerating the course of the depression.

The activities of the Reconstruction Finance Corporation allayed the panic temporarily. Whether this was merely a lull in an inevitable deflationary process or whether "the turn had come" will be forever controversial.

In accordance with the terms of a Senate resolution the Reconstruction Finance Corporation published the names of all borrowing institutions, together with the amounts they had borrowed. Whether as the result of this publicity or not a run started again in October, 1932, with the result that some 103 banks failed. Whatever confidence the people might have had in the Reconstruction Finance Corporation as an agency of recovery was now shattered. Nor did the fact that a national campaign was approaching relieve the situation. The Democrats carried Maine. This fact undoubtedly worried some of the more conservative financial interests, which, in times past at least, had been inclined to place more trust in the Republican party than in the Democratic. Hoarding was intensified, with the result that banking difficulties shortly became so acute that no relief the Reconstruction Finance Corporation could possibly extend proved adequate.

On October 31, 1932, the Lieutenant-Governor of Nevada declared a banking holiday, in connection with which he said: "The situation has at last been reached where the conditions can no longer be met by ordinary banking methods, without reorganization. It has become necessary to call upon the public to understand the problem and unite in a plan to save it."

The Iowa General Assembly, on January 20, 1933, passed a bill authorizing the State Superintendent of Banking, for a period of one year, to operate any state bank without placing it in a receivership.

On February 4, 1933, the State of Louisiana declared what was in reality a bank holiday. The State of Michigan followed on February 14th. From this time on it was only a question of days before the runs on banks everywhere became so tremendous that the banks simply could not stand the strain.

By March 1, 1933, the States of Alabama, California, Idaho, Kentucky, Louisiana, Mississippi, and Tennessee all had proclaimed bank holidays.

The pressure on the New York money market was terrific as bank after bank throughout the country called its New York balance. On March 4th the Governor of the Empire State yielded to the pressure of circumstances and closed all banks. Within twenty-four hours every state in the Union had followed suit.

President Roosevelt, on March 5th, transformed these state holidays into a national bank holiday.

The American banking system had collapsed.

CHAPTER FOUR

BANKING REFORM

THE first problem which confronted the new administration was the reopening of the banks. With an Emergency Banking Act whipped into shape and passed on March 9, 1933, the administration's attack upon the depression got under way. Under the provisions of this Banking Act the steps already taken by the administration were ratified, and further emergency powers granted. The Secretary of the Treasury was authorized to require the surrender to the Treasury of all gold coin, bullion, and gold certificates held by any individuals or corporations, in return for which an equivalent amount of any other coin or currency issued by the United States was to be paid.

The slow-moving device of receiverships was replaced by a system of conservatorships. It was hoped thereby to speed up the reorganization of these insolvent institutions. To render their reorganization even speedier, provision was made whereby the conservator might, with the consent of 75 per cent of the depositors or two-thirds of the stockholders if their equity had not been wiped out, approve any plan of reorganization which he believed "fair and equitable as to all parties concerned, and in the public interest." Such approval, incidentally, might be subjected to such conditions, restrictions, and limitations as the conservator might in his wisdom deem it wise to prescribe.

The reorganization of these institutions was still further facilitated by the provision that the conservator might, if he saw fit, authorize the issuance of non-assessable preferred stock, to bear interest at 6 per cent and to constitute a prior lien on all assets of the corporation issuing it, subject only to the claims of the depositors. Although relieved of all liability to assessment, such stock was to carry the usual voting privileges. In this fashion it was hoped, the capital structure of these various banking institutions might be strengthened. Upon the recommendation of a conservator, moreover, the Secretary of the Treasury might, with the approval of the President, request the Reconstruction Finance Corporation either to subscribe for the preferred stock of any financial institution under his control, or to advance a loan of a sufficient amount upon the basis of this collateral. The Reconstruction Finance Corporation might hold the stock thus obtained or sell it in the open market.

By far the most important section of the Emergency Banking Act, however, was that which liberalized the provisions relative to the issuance of Federal Reserve Bank notes. These bank notes were not redeemable in gold, but might, under the provisions of the law, be issued up to 100 per cent against government bonds, and up to 90 per cent against commercial paper and bankers' acceptances deposited as security. For a maximum period of two years the Reserve Banks were to make such advances, on any acceptable assets of a member bank, as were necessary. A series of amendments to the Act, passed a few days after the original enactment, extended its provisions to state banking institutions, and even authorized individuals and corporations to obtain such currency on the basis of their own promissory notes, secured by the requisite number of government bonds. This last provision was specifically designed for the benefit of areas in which banking facilities might disappear entirely under the new dispensation.

It thus became possible under the Emergency Banking Act to convert a very large percentage of the bank deposits of the country into currency.

The law passed; the task of reopening the banks began. "The Secretary of the Treasury required banks and persons having gold coins or gold certificates to turn them in at the Federal Reserve banks in exchange for other currency. Foreign-exchange operations were put under the control of the Federal Reserve members and no gold could be exported except under its license." A rapid survey of the soundness of the various banking institutions was made. For the privilege of reopening, individual banks were required to fill out applications to be filed with the respective Federal Reserve banks in the case of member institutions, and with the proper state authorities in the case of non-members. On the basis of previous examination, the information presented by the bank's management, and current examinations, these various authorities acted upon the applications thus presented. Only the solvent institutions were to be allowed to open. March 13, 1933, the reopening of the banks began, first in the Reserve cities, then in the cities which had recognized clearing-house associations, and finally, on March 15th, throughout the country.

So effective were the measures taken, confidence was immediately restored. At the end of three weeks some $15,000,000 in the new currency had been issued, and during the same period over $200,000,000 in Federal Reserve notes had been redeposited. By the middle of April approximately 75 per cent of the banking institutions of the country were going full swing, and by the middle of August 13,951 banks, holding approximately 94 per cent of the deposits of the country, were open on an unrestricted basis.

The banking crisis was over.

Although the Emergency Banking Act took care of the banking crisis, it did little or nothing to correct those defects of management and organization which had contributed so largely to the débâcle. True, approximately 3,000 banks did not open, or opened under a conservator. To the extent that these weak units were eliminated from our banking system some improvement had been attained; the basic defects, nevertheless, remained. Unit banking was to characterize the future as it had the past. Nothing had been done to rectify the shift in policy from commercial to investment banking. Nor had the issuance of preferred stock by various banking institutions and its purchase by the Reconstruction Finance Corporation been without disadvantage, for such action had undoubtedly bolstered many a weak institution which might better, from the standpoint of our banking organization, have been allowed to go to the wall.

On June 16, 1933, the Glass-Steagall bill was passed. Through its provisions an attempt was made to correct some of the more basic defects of the past. Through a Federal guarantee of deposits an attempt was made to entice money back from hoarding, and to end forever the possibility of a stampede such as that which led to the collapse. Through the divorce of security affiliates from their parent institutions, and the prohibition of the receipt of demand deposits by investment banking houses, an attempt was made to correct the confusion which had arisen in banking circles as to the functions of investment and commercial banks. Additional powers of supervision designed to curb the speculative use of credit, were given the Federal Reserve Board. The admission of Morris Plan banks, mutual savings-banks, and security institutions into membership in the Reserve System, in the same manner and subject to the same provisions of law as state banks and trust companies, was intended to strengthen the banking community through further centralization and supervision. The permission accorded Reserve member banks to establish statewide branches, within every state giving similar permission to its own banks, had a similar objective. It was hoped thus to entice into joining the Reserve System many state banks which by virtue of their ownership of branch banks had hitherto remained outside. It made possible, furthermore, an expansion of the activities of Federal Reserve banks heretofore illegal. Moreover, the deposit-guarantee system, although having as its primary purpose the restoration of confidence in the banking system, may have as its incidental consequence the bringing of every bank in the country into the Reserve System. It is difficult to imagine any other result from adoption of the guarantee system than the gradual transfer of deposits from banks not members of the system to those which are.

Thus, although the new legislation does not eliminate or, for that matter, radically reduce unit banking, it does contain several features which in the long run may drastically modify American banking organization and practices. In no way, however, did the Glass-Steagall bill contribute to the further liquidation of post-war inflation. That it did not do so was inevitable, for, as we shall have occasion to point out again and again in the course of our analysis, an underlying assumption of the Recovery Program is that the evils of post-war inflation had been more than adequately corrected in the days between the stock-market crash and March 4, 1933. Indeed, it was the consensus of opinion that the deflation had gone too far.

The deposit-guarantee feature of the Glass-Steagall bill is without question its most controversial aspect. The plan was not altogether new in America, for after the panic of 1907 a number of states in the Middle West adopted statewide deposit-guarantee schemes of one form or another, all of which it might be said incidentally failed. Their failure for the most part is traceable to the fact that each of the states which engaged in the undertaking was predominantly agricultural in its economy; therefore no adequate distribution of risk was possible. Nor was the problem of administration satisfactorily solved. "Personal and political favoritism was common. Banks took speculative risks; if they turned out well there were great profits for the bankers; if there were losses, they came out of the state fund."

Despite this history—perhaps because of this history—a limited guarantee of bank deposits was written into the Federal law. Under its provisions a Federal Deposit Insurance Corporation was instituted, headed by a board of directors appointed by the President, subject to the confirmation of the Senate.

The first task of the new Corporation was the creation of a Temporary Federal Deposit Insurance Fund. Membership in this Fund was obligatory upon every bank which was a member of the Federal Reserve System, open and licensed to operate on or before January 1, 1934. Non-member banks whose solvency was unquestionable might also become members of the Fund.

The first problem confronting the directors of the

Corporation, consequently, was the determination of the solvency of the institutions making application for membership. Although the burden of determining the financial condition of the members of the Federal Reserve System fell upon the Comptroller of the Treasury and the Federal Reserve Board, the task of passing upon the application of the 8,000 and more non-member banks which applied for membership was in itself an onerous one. Almost over night a staff had to be whipped into shape. Offices had to be opened here and there throughout the country, and a Board of Review set up.

Down to date the Corporation has insisted on a ratio of at least 10 per cent of capital to deposit liability as the *sine qua non* of membership in the Fund. Only thus has it seemed possible to provide an adequate cushion for the risk the Corporation is undertaking.[1]

When an application has been received from an institution in which such a ratio between capital structure and deposits does not exist, the directors of the Corporation have urged the bankers concerned to raise the additional capital locally, or, if that is not possible, to make application to the Reconstruction Finance Corporation for a capital loan. As a result of this policy the Reconstruction Finance Corporation had, up to and including February 9, 1934 made available, or entered into conditional agreement to make available, to some 5,953 banks both state and national, funds in an aggregate of $984,830,850. Approximately $40,000,000, it might be said incidentally, has been raised locally. Thus the capital structure of our banking system has been strengthened enormously, and

1 Whether the assets of the various banks are being carried at a sufficiently conservative figure to warrant complete confidence in the administration of the funds is even now a moot question.

the Deposit Insurance Fund has been launched, so it is maintained, on a comparatively sound basis. (Whether the fact that the preferred stock so purchased has a preferred claim upon all assets of the bank, subject to the claims of the depositors, renders it a reasonably secure investment for the Reconstruction Finance Corporation is, perhaps, a moot question. It may well be that, although the Federal Deposit Insurance Corporation has thus been put on a sound basis, the Reconstruction Finance Corporation may, nevertheless, take tremendous losses.)

With the aid the Reconstruction Finance Corporation has thus extended, 13,870 banks have at the present writing become members of the Temporary Reserve Fund. In other words, 91 per cent of all the banks in the country eligible for membership in the Temporary Federal Deposit Insurance Fund have applied for membership and been accepted. Application for admission on the part of members of the Federal Reserve System was of course obligatory. Nevertheless, they represent only 45 per cent of the total membership of the Fund. At the present time, consequently, the Federal Deposit Insurance Corporation has insured 55.6 million accounts, covering 37½ per cent of the total deposits of the country—nearly $16,000,000,000.

To cover the obligations thus assumed, a fund of some $320,000,000, drawn from three main sources has been established. A subscription from the Treasury totals $150,000,000; one from the Federal Reserve Banks $135,000,000; and an assessment on the member banks brings the fund to this grand total. Incidentally, a second assessment of some $40,000,000 upon the member banks is provided for, should occasion arise.

In reply to the query as to whether this sum, vast as it

is, is adequate coverage for the enormous funds insured, the directors of the Corporation point out that there is in this sum a coverage of 2 per cent in contrast to an average coverage maintained by Lloyds of only 1 per cent.

Down to date, after six months of operation, only two members of the Federal Deposit Insurance Corporation have closed their doors. This is in striking contrast to the monthly record of the decade preceding, when fifty or more bank failures a month was the usual thing.[2]

The second task of the Federal Deposit Insurance Corporation is the establishment of a Permanent Federal Deposit Insurance Fund with a capital structure of approximately half a billion dollars. This fund, like the temporary one, is to come from three main sources. First, a $150,000,000 subscription from the Treasury; second, the purchase by the federal reserve banks of Class B stock in the Corporation to the amount of one-half their surpluses as of January 1, 1933—approximately $135,000,000; and third, the purchase of Class A 6 per cent non-voting cumulative stock by member banks and such non-member banks as have been members of the Temporary Fund to the extent of one-half of one per cent of their deposit liabilities. Incidentally, those latter banks must become members of the Federal Reserve System by or before July 1, 1936.

[2] A cynic might, of course, remark that for a bank to fail in these times, with the Reconstruction Finance Corporation standing ready to pour hundreds of thousands, if not millions, of dollars into its capital structure, is almost an impossibility. The recent failures might be taken, consequently, as conclusive evidence that the age of miracles has not passed. Such a comment would, nevertheless, be exceedingly unfair, for it fails to take into account the fact that the activities of the Reconstruction Finance Corporation in strengthening the capital structure of these various banking institutions is part and parcel of the general inflationary program to which the administration is committed.

Under the Permanent Fund deposits up to $10,000 are guaranteed in full. Deposits between $10,000 and $50,000 are guaranteed only to 75 per cent of their book value; and deposits over $50,000 only to 50 per cent of their book value. Whether the Permanent Deposit Fund will ever go into operation remains to be seen. The officers of the Federal Deposit Insurance Corporation are opposed to it. And at their suggestion the life of the Temporary Fund has been continued for another year, with the limit of the deposits guaranteed in full raised to $5,000.

The opposition of the directors of the Federal Deposit Insurance Corporation to the Permanent Insurance Fund in its present form rests upon the fact (a) that as the law now stands in many states, it would be impossible for many mutual savings-banks, now members of the Temporary Insurance Fund, to transfer their membership to the Permanent Fund; (b) that it would be virtually impossible for the Comptroller of the Currency or the Federal Reserve Banks, in the time allotted, to make the examination of the member institutions required by law; and (c) that the powers of supervision now given to the Federal Deposit Insurance Corporation are negligible. Whether the Federal Deposit Insurance Corporation will avoid the pitfalls of its state predecessors, time alone can tell.

Another feature of the law which deserves comment relates to the handling of closed banks. The procedure differs radically from anything which preceded it. Briefly summarized, the law provides that in the event of the failure of a national bank, a new national bank is to be formed immediately. The new institution need have neither directors nor capital. It is, instead, to be directly under the administration of the Federal Deposit Insurance Corporation. The money due the depositors of the old national bank from the insurance fund is to be turned over —not to the depositors—but to the new national bank, where it is to be at the disposal of the depositors as it would be in any other bank. The obvious hope of the legislative architect responsible for drafting this section of the bill is that the depositors will allow their money to remain in the new bank. Thus the community involved may avoid the inconvenience of an even temporarily suspended banking service. The new bank is to be run by the Federal Deposit Insurance Corporation on a limited basis until such time as the Corporation can find individuals who are willing to subscribe the necessary capital for the new institution, at which time the management will, of course, be turned over to them. If the Corporation is unsuccessful in obtaining the necessary capital, however, it may, after due notice, sell the bank to another bank. Failing either to secure the necessary capital or to find a purchaser, the Corporation may, after two years, put the bank through a voluntary liquidation.

A similar procedure is to be followed in the case of state banks where the state law permits. It is hoped thus to eliminate some of the defects inherent in the slower moving device of a bank receivership.

CHAPTER FIVE

THE MONETARY POLICY

Inextricably tied up with the banking policy of the Roosevelt administration is its much controverted monetary policy. Under the authority of an Act originally passed October 9, 1917, usually known as the Trading with the Enemy Act, President Roosevelt proclaimed a bank holiday, March 6, 1933, in connection with which he prohibited any bank from paying out, exporting, earmarking or permitting the withdrawal or transfer in any manner whatsoever, of any gold or silver coin or bullion or currency, or taking any other action which might facilitate the hoarding thereof. This action was, of course, dictated by the fear that, once the banks had reopened, a revival of the run on gold might take place. And although it was possible, as we have already discovered, to erect a currency system whereby practically all the deposits of the country could, if necessary, be converted into currency, it was simply impossible to cover these deposits with gold. An inevitable corollary was the prohibition on shipments of gold abroad. This, as Paul Warburg has pointed out, was a political necessity, since the American people would have had great difficulty in understanding why they themselves could not obtain gold if it could be shipped abroad. On March 10th, consequently, the export of gold was definitely forbidden.

The day before, as we have already observed, the

Emergency Banking Act was passed. Previous to the passage of this Act most of our currency was buttressed with a 40-per-cent gold reserve. With the passage of this Act, Federal Reserve bank notes backed only by government bonds, notes, drafts, bills of exchange, and bankers' acceptances, could be pumped into circulation as circumstances demanded. Although this was not, in a sense, an inflationary measure, since no positive steps were taken to pump money into circulation, it was nevertheless an extremely liberal currency policy.[1]

Synchronous with the Proclamation of March 6th was the launching of the drive against gold hoarding. No definitive action was taken, however, until April 5th, when President Roosevelt issued an order requiring all holders of gold or gold certificates "to deliver the same to a Federal Reserve bank or a member bank by May 1st in exchange for other currency. . . . Gold ear-marked for foreign governments, central banks, or the Bank for International Settlements, gold for industrial use, collectors' coins, and $100 per person, however, were exempted." The drive against the gold-hoarders was renewed from time to time, but only one actual prosecution for hoarding was instituted. Just what this action on the part of the administration signified was, in the beginning, not very clear. The original order was "justified on the ground that gold in private hoards served no useful purpose, but in the Federal Reserve banks it could be used as a basis for currency and credit and so promote recovery."

On April 20, 1933, the issuance of an Executive Order

[1] One of the first positive steps taken to increase the circulation of money was the purchase, by the Reconstruction Finance Corporation of shares of preferred stock in our various banking institutions, to which I have already referred.

Relating to Foreign Exchange and the Ear-marking and Exports of Gold Coin, Bullion or Currency made it clear that we had gone off the gold standard not merely for the emergency, but for some time to come.

Almost simultaneously with the issuance of this order the President requested his advisers to draft a series of amendments to the Agricultural Adjustment Act combining into one measure, permissive in character, the various and sundry inflationary proposals then before Congress. This legislation was embodied in the Agricultural Adjustment Act and the amendments thereto which were enacted into law on May 12, 1933. Briefly summarized, these amendments provided that whenever the President upon investigation shall find that "(1) the foreign commerce of the United States is adversely affected by reason of the depreciation in the value of the currency of any other government or governments in relation to the present standard value of gold, or (2) action under this section is necessary in order to regulate and maintain the parity of currency issues of the United States, or (3) an economic emergency requires the expansion of credit, or (4) an expansion of credit is necessary to secure any international agreement on stabilization at proper levels of the currencies of various governments," he may in his discretion persuade the Federal Reserve Banks to conduct open market operations in the obligations of the United States to a maximum of $3,000,000,000 without reference either to their reserve requirements or discount rates.

If, however, the Reserve Banks are unwilling or unable to cooperate, the President may then direct the Treasury to issue United States notes (greenbacks) to a total of $3,000,000,000. These are to be exchanged for United States government bonds or other interest-bearing obligations, and must be retired at the rate of 4 per cent a year. Alternately, the President is empowered to fix the weight of the gold dollar at not less than 50 per cent of its weight at the time the Agricultural Adjustment Act was passed. He may also, unless I misinterpret the law, establish a bimetallic system, fixing the relative weight of both gold and silver, and provide for the unlimited coinage of each. Furthermore, for a period of six months following the passage of the Act the President is, or rather was, authorized to accept silver from foreign governments in payment of their indebtedness to the United States up to a total of $200,000,000 at a price of not more than fifty cents an ounce. Against any silver which might thus be acquired, silver certificates, of an amount equal to the valuation set upon the silver taken in payment of debts, were to be issued.

In this fashion was the stage set for inflation.

The concluding paragraph of the act provides, however, that "the Federal Reserve Board, upon the affirmative vote of not less than five of its members, and with the approval of the President, may declare that an emergency exists by reason of credit expansion, and may, by regulation during such emergency, increase or decrease from time to time, in its discretion, the reserve balances required to be maintained against either demand or time deposits."

Thus an emergency brake was added to our financial machine.

Were these amendments merely part of the game of politics, designed to head off a radical inflation or had the President been converted to the theories of the inflationists? This was the question discussed far and wide throughout the country. Not even the President's defense of the repudiation of the gold clause contained in the bonds of the United States, and his proclamation in the course of a radio address on May 7th, of his intention to raise prices entirely ended the uncertainty.

One question clearly needed clarification,—the legality of the clause, frequently found in both public and private bonds, providing for the payment of principal and interest "in gold coin of the present degree of weight and fineness." Had this clause been universally abrogated when we went off the gold standard, or were business concerns and governmental units legally committed to do the illegal?—the impossible? A joint resolution of Congress, approved by the President on June 5th, 1933, declared the fulfillment of all existing "gold clause" contracts to be against public policy, and specifically authorized the payment of all obligations containing such a stipulation in any form of legal tender.

In his speech of May 7th, to which I have already referred, President Roosevelt had said:

"The administration has the definite objective of raising commodity prices to such an extent that those who have borrowed money will, on the average, be able to repay that money in the same kind of dollar they borrowed."

The inflationary amendments to the Agricultural Adjustment Act were obviously designed to enable him to carry out that purpose.

Despite the fact that the conversations preceding the World Monetary and Economic Conference which opened in London on June 12, 1933, revealed a divergence quite fundamental in character between the "gold bloc" and the British, and a still further divergence between the "gold bloc," the British and the United States, plans for the Conference were laid. Assistant Secretary of

State Moley, with this divergence primarily in mind, indicated in a radio address as early as May 20th that little or nothing might come from the Conference. Events were to prove he was right. But even he seemingly did not realize how rapidly the President was coming to accept the point of view of the inflationists, to wit that inflation alone could produce the requisite rise in the price level.

So deep was the rift between the "gold bloc" and the countries which had left the gold standard, that at the time of Mr. Moley's arrival in London the Conference seemed to be on the point of breaking up. An attempt was made to forestall such an eventuality through the formulation of a statement which declared for "stability in the international monetary field" and the "reestablishment of gold as the measure of international exchange value" as soon as practicable. Each nation, however, was left to determine for itself the exact date upon which it would return to gold. Innocuous though the statement was, endorsed though it was by Mr. Roosevelt's closest adviser, the President repudiated it in emphatic terms. More important than the force of his repudiation was the fact that he committed himself to a monetary policy which made the working out of an international agreement impossible. He said, in effect, that thenceforth the United States would "no longer be concerned with the foreign-exchange value of the dollar, but rather with the purchasing power of the dollar in terms of the American price level." He announced definitely that the primary preoccupation of the American government would be "to raise the price level in this country"; that nothing would "be permitted to stand in the way of the attainment of this objective"; and that "once the desired price level had been reached it would be established."

As a consequence of Mr. Roosevelt's message to the World Economic Conference, the Conference found itself in such an impasse that it went into an indefinite recess with only one accomplishment to its credit.[2] At no time during the summer, however, did the President reveal what his monetary policy actually was. The dollar was simply permitted to drift.

The effect of its drifting seemingly was exceedingly satisfactory. On July 18th, the dollar having fallen to sixty-nine cents, wheat, which in April had been selling at sixty-eight cents, had risen to $1.24; cotton was selling at just about twice its price the previous February; stocks had more than doubled their averages.

Then came a crash. Prices finally began once more to recover, but very slowly. And still the administration took no positive action. "Large open-market purchases of government securities were made by the Federal Reserve, but on its own initiative rather than that of the Treasury." The Agricultural Adjustment Administration, the National Recovery Administration, and the Public Works Administration were the agencies upon which the administration was leaning, rather than upon monetary manipulation, in its determination to force prices up.

Prices did rise. But in October there came another collapse. Three courses were now possible—stabilization, the direct use of greenbacks, or a depreciation of foreign exchange.

In a radio address on October 22, 1933, again affirming his determination to raise commodity prices, the Presi-

[2] The subcommittee on permanent measures recommended an agreement on silver whereby any debasement of silver coins below a fineness of 800/1000 would be prohibited and whereby silver coins would be substituted for notes of smaller denominations.

dent expressed his dissatisfaction with the progress which had been made thus far and announced the gold-purchase plan. "My aim in taking this step," he said, "is to establish and maintain continuous control. This is a policy and not an expedient. We are thus continuing to move toward a managed currency." On October 25th the new policy went into effect. The price of gold was fixed at $31.36 an ounce as against $29.80 on the previous day. Thereafter the price was gradually raised until on December 18th it was $34.06. Not only was the active domestic supply of gold thus absorbed, but by December 21st some $50,000,000 had been bought abroad. The gold-purchase plan was, in so far as the public knows, largely sponsored by Professor Warren of Cornell and Professor James Harvey Rogers of Yale.

An analysis of the works of these advisers, consequently, may perhaps reveal the theoretical reasoning behind the procedure. "The basic theory which apparently underlies the new policy is, stated in its simplest terms, that the price level is directly related to the value of gold. Gold is regarded as a world commodity, and its value in terms of goods is, therefore, determined by world supply in relation to world demand. Hence the value of gold, or the amount of goods which exchanges for a given weight of gold, tends to be the same in every country. If the supply of gold increases faster than the demand for gold, its value will fall, and this means (assuming no change in the commodity situation) that each ounce of gold will then exchange for a smaller quantity of other goods than before. Putting the matter another way, more gold would have to be offered for the same quantity of commodities and the price level would rise everywhere." [3]

[3] Leo Pasvolsky, *Current Monetary Issues*, p. 107.

A second line of argument in support of the gold-purchase plan is that its immediate effect will be—perhaps I should say, has been—the depreciation of the dollar on the foreign exchange. This obviously means an increase in the price of imported goods. Similarly, all other things remaining the same, the depreciation of the American dollar should mean an increase in our export trade. In terms of European currencies American goods can now be purchased at much lower prices than formerly. In consequence, an increased demand should be forthcoming, and as a result of this increased demand, the prices of those commodities which go into our export trade should (the supply remaining the same) increase. Moreover, this increase, over a long period of time should exert an indirect effect on the whole price level.

How sound is the reasoning behind the gold-purchase plan? The answer to the question will depend upon whether you are an adherent of the Warren school of economic thought or a devotee of the more orthodox sects of economic reasoning. It is within the realm of probability that the depreciation of the dollar abroad has had some effect upon our export trade, and thus indirectly upon the price level. Nevertheless, to attribute any large proportion of the price rise which has occurred during the last eighteen months to the gold-purchase plan would be dubious logic indeed.

Whether, because of dissatisfaction with the results of the gold-purchase plan or because of necessities of a political nature, on December 21, 1933, the President announced the ratification of the international silver agreement, and at the same time inaugurated a program of buying newly mined silver. By buying newly mined domestic silver at sixty-four and one-half cents an ounce as over against a market price of forty-three and one-half cents, a handsome sop was thrown to the silver miners. Whether anything more than this was accomplished is yet to be seen.

With the opening of the recent session of the seventy-third Congress some definitive statement by the President relative to his monetary policy was anticipated. Shortly after the opening of Congress Mr. Roosevelt sent his monetary message. Briefly summarized, it recommended three things: "(1) that all gold be taken over by the Treasury, (2) that the limits of revaluation be fixed between 50 and 60 per cent of the old dollar, and (3) that a large part of the 'profit' due to revaluing gold be set aside as a stabilization fund, to steady the dollar and the national credit."

The Gold Reserve bill was sent to the President for his approval on January 30, 1934. A day later Mr. Roosevelt issued a proclamation devaluing the dollar to 59.06 per cent of its old par value, a figure which was arrived at by fixing the price of gold at $35 an ounce.

A stabilization fund of two billion dollars was created "by setting aside much of the 'profit' we made through revaluing the gold stocks of the Treasury and the Federal Reserve System." The fund is in the hands of the Secretary of the Treasury to use "in his sole discretion." Just what has been, or is being done with the fund is not at the moment public knowledge.

On April 10, 1934, the administration took further action. Something more had to be done for silver. In consequence, there was formulated the Silver Purchase Act, which declared it to be the policy of the United States to increase the silver holdings of the government until such time as the monetary stocks of the country shall be made up of silver and gold in the ratio of one to three.

It authorized the Secretary of the Treasury "to purchase silver, at home or abroad, for present or future delivery, at such rates and times and upon such terms as he may deem reasonable and most advantageous to the United States; provided that no purchase of silver shall be made at a price in excess of its monetary value, and that no purchase of silver situated in the United States on May 1, 1934, shall be at a price in excess of fifty cents a fine ounce."

Against the silver so bought, silver certificates are to be issued to the full value of the silver accumulated. The recent order relative to the nationalization of all silver within the United States is merely a further step in carrying out the provisions of the law. What will be done with the silver once it has been accumulated is as yet unknown.

Whatever one may think of the details of the administration's monetary policies, however, one fact is certain—they have one and all been inflationary in character. Although the price level which the administration is seeking to attain has not yet been reached, I, for one at least, do not believe it is possible for the administration to continue to take step after step in the direction in which it is going without the effect being felt sooner or later. Each step which has been taken has been taken with such caution that it seems improbable that we in the United States will, as the orthodox economists have from time to time suggested, be confronted with a runaway inflation of the German variety. It remains to be seen, however, whether the administration will, with the rapidity and delicacy which will be necessary, be able to control rising prices once their actions have taken effect, so that the rising cost of living will not inflict as great a hardship on the fixed income group as did the deflation upon the debtors.

CHAPTER SIX

SECURITIES

ONLY slightly less important than the problem of money and banking is that of securities. That a radical change in the method of floating securities and in the operation of the security exchanges was imperative had been clearly indicated by several investigations in the course of the depression. The demand for public regulation was insistent. In consequence of this demand a Securities Act was passed, May 27, 1933, forbidding the transportation in interstate commerce of any securities, or prospectus offering securities for sale, unless the said securities, or prospectus, as the case might be, had previously been registered with the Federal Trade Commission.[1]

The registration of each such prospectus was "to be accomplished by the filing of a statement signed by the principal officers and a majority of the board of directors of the issuing company, and in the case of foreign issues by the authorized representative of the issues in the United States." The items of information called for ranged from the names and addresses of the directors of the corporation to a full analysis of the capital structure of the corporation issuing the securities. The purpose of the information thus demanded was, of course, the protection of the investor. By virtue of the additional data

1 The administration of the Securities Act has since been transferred to the Securities and Exchange Commission. See page 54.

thus made available it was hoped that a sounder judgment might be exercised by the investing public in the future than had been exercised in the past.

Should any item of information in the registration statement prove false, the Federal Trade Commission is empowered to suspend the registration. Moreover, any such falsification may form the basis of suit by any person who has acquired such a security in good faith against every signer of the registration statement, every director of the issuing company, every engineer, accountant, appraiser, or underwriter who has consented to be named in connection with the issue—to the full amount paid for the security. Moreover, a fine of not more than $5,000, imprisonment for not more than five years, or both may be imposed.

It should be stated parenthetically, perhaps, that the Act did not apply to "securities offered or issued within sixty days after the passage of the Act, or to securities of the United States, local or state governments, national or state banks, commercial paper, securities of religious, educational, charitable, fraternal, or reformatory corporations, building or loan associations, savings-banks and similar institutions, railroad securities, certificates issued by receivers or insurance policies."

Hardly had the Securities Act been passed when a storm of criticism broke. The chief barrage was leveled at the penalties imposed. Again and again it was asserted that the Act imposed cruel and unusual punishments for what, after all, might be honest mistakes; that so long as it was on the statute-books, no new securities could be issued; that no reputable investment house would subject itself to the penalties of such a law. The issuance of new securities did in fact, dwindle to practically nothing.

Whether this concerted action, or rather inaction, on the part of the investment houses was, as certain writers have asserted, a form of sabotage, or whether the investment houses were honestly afraid to take the risks under the law will remain always a moot question.

As a result of the criticisms a number of amendments were made to the Act by the second session of the seventy-third Congress, amendments which have, in the opinion of the legal advisers of the leading investment houses, "removed many of the difficulties previously in the way of issuing new securities." Whether they have not also removed much of the protection previously accorded to the investor remains to be seen.

That some share of responsibility for the tragedy of 1929 rests upon the stock exchanges of the country is almost incontrovertible. Far from taking effective steps to check the orgy of speculation, the brokerage houses outdid Monte Carlo in their efforts to stimulate the gambling. To render the recurrence of a similar catastrophe less likely in the future the Securities Exchange Act of 1934 was passed, and a bipartizan Securities and Exchange Commission of five members, appointed by the President by and with the consent of the Senate, was established. Under its jurisdiction fell both the Securities Exchange Act and the Securities Act.

To the end that excessive speculation and unethical stock practices may be eliminated the Commission is authorized to require the registration both of the exchanges and of all listed securities. Needless to say the contents of these registration statements may be modified from time to time as the Commission may dictate. And in addition periodic reports, certified by independent public accountants, may be required from each and every corporation whose securities are listed on the exchanges. The functions of dealers, brokers, and specialists are carefully defined, and specific manipulative practices designed to establish artificial prices are to be penalized. Furthermore, a fine of $10,000, two years' imprisonment, or both, may be imposed for any violation of the provisions of the Act. Where an exchange is a violator a maximum penalty of $500,000 is possible.

In addition, the Securities and Exchange Commission, together with the Federal Reserve Board, may regulate margin requirements and brokers' credits. The Federal Reserve Board is empowered to prescribe rules and regulations with respect to the amount of credit that may be initially extended and subsequently maintained on any other than exempted securities, and is also empowered to raise or lower such requirements as it sees fit. The Act specifically provides, however, that "an amount not greater than whichever is the higher of—(1) 55 per cent of the current market price, or (2) 100 per cent of the lowest market price of the security during the preceding thirty-six months, but not more than 75 per cent of the current market price," shall constitute the standard margin requirement.

Thus at least an attempt has been made to prevent a recurrence in the future of the perversion of credit which has characterized the past.

CHAPTER SEVEN

THE R. F. C.

To AN extent which is true of no other agency of the administration the activities of the Reconstruction Finance Corporation are inextricably interwoven with the whole recovery program. Created June 22, 1932, under the Hoover administration, it has under President Roosevelt become the great credit reservoir of the new administration. Launched originally with a capital of $500,000,000 and authority to issue bonds to a total of $1,500,000, its authority has been expanded so that today its borrowing power is well over $7,500,000,000. With this money it has been attempting to buttress the economic position of various segments of our economy in such a way as to prevent a major economic failure. The purpose of its activities is not, needless to say, to promote the welfare of this or that group of stockholders, but rather to prevent a major failure in our economic order which in and of itself might start once again the downward spiral of economic forces.

To this end it has loaned money to and purchased stock from railroads, financial institutions, insurance companies, building and loan associations, etc., etc., to a total of $5,538,000,000. Of this amount some $1,517,000,000 has already been paid back, so the balance outstanding at the close of the fiscal year, June 30, 1934, was $4,021,000,000.

A recent amendment to the Act increasing the borrowing power of the Reconstruction Finance Corporation by some $580,000,000 is designed to enable it to extend loans to small industries thus tiding them over the initial stages of the recovery.

Whether the Reconstruction Finance Corporation will be able to withdraw the funds it has thus loaned, or whether the activities of this Corporation mark a transition to state capitalism or, perhaps, to state socialism, is something which still lies behind the curtain of Time. Should its activities really mark a transitional stage, as some writers assert, responsibility will have to be laid at the door of circumstances rather than upon any preconceived idea of the legislative architects of the Corporation.

CHAPTER EIGHT

THE BUDGET

EQUALLY important with the other fiscal problems here being discussed is the problem of the budget. Sooner or later debts must either be paid or repudiated.

On coming into office March 4, 1933, Mr. Roosevelt was faced with an already accumulated deficit as of June 30, 1932, of $2,885,400,000. And in view of the fact that the expenditures already authorized for the fiscal year 1932-33 were something over $3,158,000,000, whereas the anticipated revenues totaled little less than $2,280,000,000, an increase in this deficit could certainly be anticipated.

In the course of his campaign Mr. Roosevelt had pledged drastic economies. Four days after taking office, he renewed his pledge and asked for authority to deal with the emergency. This led to the passage of the Economy Act, under whose provisions the President was given almost *carte blanche* in dealing with both the pension system, and government salaries, although reductions in this latter category were limited to 15 per cent. In addition he was given authority to reorganize the administrative set-up of the Federal service in such a way as to introduce increased efficiencies and to attain greater economies. By virtue of this authority an executive order was issued on March 28th, reducing all administrative salaries in the Federal service 15 per cent, effecting thereby an estimated savings of between $350,000,000 and $400,000,000. A week or two later came another order revising the pension system, effecting a saving of an additional $400,000,000. The consolidation of administrative agencies and the elimination of so-called unnecessary services it was hoped would bring the savings thus effected to the grand total of $1,000,000,000.

If the budget was to be balanced, however, new revenues were still necessary.

To this end the beer bill was passed, the gasoline tax increased; an excess-profits tax imposed; the provisions of the income tax were tightened up; and a number of other efforts were made to increase revenues.

By this time, however, the broad outlines of the recovery program had been formulated. The choice had been made between deflation and reflation.

It became evident very shortly that it would be impossible to follow a reflationary program and pursue a pay-as-you-go policy at one and the same time. To levy taxes to a total of one-third of the national income was a political impossibility. Logically or illogically, the decision to formulate two budgets was therefore made,—an ordinary budget for the usual expenditures of government, and an extraordinary budget for the emergency expenditures. The argument was advanced that only the ordinary budget need be kept in balance in the orthodox sense of that term. The extraordinary budget might well be considered to be balanced if provision was made to meet the interest and amortization charges on the bonds issued. Later in the year all pretense at maintaining a balanced budget was abandoned.

In consequence of the recovery program the national debt, which had been reduced from a peak of $26,594,-

000,000 to some $16,185,000,000 and had then risen to over $20,000,000,000, is now something over $27,000,-000,000. In 1933-34 alone expenditures totaled $7,105,-000,000 as against receipts of $3,116,000,000. Nor is the end in sight. Forecasts for the coming year indicate an expenditure of approximately $10,000,000,000 as against receipts of less than $5,000,000,000.

How serious this situation appears to the reader will depend, of course, upon his economic philosophy. Nevertheless, the fact that Great Britain, with a much smaller population and much less wealth to draw on, manages to stagger along under a public debt of approximately $32,-000,000,000 indicates that there is no immediate cause for hysteria. Sooner or later, however, the budget must be balanced.

AGRICULTURE

CHAPTER NINE

THE FARM REVOLT

A JUDGE dragged from his bench, foreclosure sales halted, a farmers' holiday, a wheat embargo, roads picketed, milk dumped—this was the news from the farm front, where the embattled farmers stood, once again firing shots heard 'round the world.

Should it have been taken seriously, or was it merely the stage thunder of politicians attempting to exploit the farmers for their own selfish purposes? Whether the "hell-raisers" were responsible for this particular action or that, the fact remains that their activities were symptomatic of an unrest which had pervaded the farming communities for more than a decade. That each and every farmer was on the verge of starvation was obviously untrue. That the bulk of our agricultural community was in anything like the dire distress of the vast army of unemployed was also open to challenge.

Nevertheless, one thing was certain. Farmer after farmer had lost his life savings and his farm because he had not been able to meet the payments on his mortgage. Farmer after farmer had been evicted from his home and added to the ranks of the unemployed because he had not been able to pay his taxes. And thousands of others lived constantly in fear of a visit from the sheriff.

This is the explanation of the farm revolt. So unfair had the working of our legal, economic system seemed at times—a system which dispossessed from their homes honest, hard-working men who, through no apparent fault of their own, had been unable to meet their legal obligations—that an outraged sense of decency and justice had impelled friends and neighbors to come to their assistance irrespective of the legality of their actions. In part the farmer had been caught in the same economic cycle in which the rest of us were involved; in part his predicament was and is unique.

The factors which have contributed to the farmer's plight fall, for the most part, into four categories: overproduction, loss of foreign markets, diminution of demand in the domestic markets, and excessively high fixed operating charges. The American farmer was simply producing more of the staple commodities than could be consumed under the present system of distribution.

This was partly due to the tremendous improvement in agricultural machinery which has been effected during the last fifty years. Two acres may now be cultivated where but one could have been tilled before. Hillsides which previously could be cropped only with the greatest difficulty have long since been brought under the plow. Moreover, scientific knowledge in connection with agriculture has advanced by leaps and bounds. A more effective use of fertilizers, a more careful selection of seeds, a more extensive and intensive use of insecticides have all contributed to heavier and heavier crops per acre.

Equally significant, is the fact that the undeveloped portions of the earth's surface have within recent years been rapidly brought under cultivation. The agricultural surpluses of the so-called backward nations have in consequence increased enormously, while international competition has become more and more intense.

The sum total result of all these factors has been overproduction at home and abroad. American wheat and American cotton no longer dominate the world markets. This is due in part to the ever-increasing surpluses of wheat produced in Canada, Australia, and the Argentine; in part to increased cotton production in both India and Egypt.

The shift in the position of America from a debtor nation—owing money to the creditor nations of Europe—to a creditor nation—owed by all, has likewise complicated the situation. While we were a debtor nation, the creditor nations of Europe were willing, indeed anxious, to receive our agricultural products in payment of both the interest and principal of the money we owed them. With the change in our status, these creditor nations no longer feel the same necessity for receiving our surpluses. Quite the contrary! They deem it wise economy to enter into trade compacts with other nations which today owe them money so that through the surpluses they may make collections from these debtor nations. This explains, in part at least, the trade agreement between England and her Dominions, and between England and the Argentine.

The American tariff policy was, perhaps, the final factor contributing to the collapse of our foreign markets, agricultural and industrial alike. It provoked first protests, then retaliation. European tariff rates were raised against us. A quota system was established. This alone might have sufficed to account for the diminution of our foreign trade. Whatever the weight of these several items, the American farmer had, in fact, lost the larger share of his export trade, and equally important—for what he did export he received totally inadequate compensation.

The radical transformation of our system of transportation as a factor in the diminution of the demand for agricultural products in the domestic market has frequently been overlooked. The automobile and the tractor have replaced the horse and the mule. In the process, they have undoubtedly developed a demand for steel, gasoline, and other basic commodities. But, unfortunately, so far as the grain farmer is concerned, they have reduced tremendously the markets for his oats. Old Dobbin was a faithful friend in more ways than one.

Similarly, prohibition had affected the farmer's domestic market. "Ostrolenk estimates that the Eighteenth Amendment destroyed an annual market for 65,000,000 bushels of barley, 33,000,000 bushels of corn, and 35,000,000 bushels of hops, a total twice as great as our whole export of those commodities in 1925." Whether these estimates are correct or not, it is interesting to recall that one of the arguments for prohibition in the days when "food will win the war" was a familiar slogan, was the savings of foodstuffs it would effect.

The change in eating habits in America was also an element in the situation which should not be overlooked. The "cult of the boyish form" may have made America a more pleasant place in which to live. It did, nevertheless, contribute to the farmer's dilemma.

Nor had the transition from voluminous cottons to scanty silks been without its consequence.

Most important by far, however, among the factors accentuating the crisis in agriculture was the crash of our industrial system and the rise of a vast army of unemployed. Not choice, but necessity, dictated a curtailment of their demands. And that this curtailment seriously affected the farmer's domestic market was and is too obvious to need comment. A radical fall in agricultural prices was inevitable. Had all other prices fallen similarly, the drop in agricultural prices might not have been so significant. Unfortunately, such was not the case. Many prices remained fixed; others fell only slightly. Semi-monopolistic industries, with huge surpluses upon which to draw, did not feel the pressure to cut prices as did the individualistic farmer.

Taxes remained approximately the same. Hard-surfaced roads, county-fair grounds, centralized schoolhouses, built in the days of prosperity, still had to be paid for. Interest and amortization charges remained the same. These charges which once seemed so reasonable now seemed crushingly onerous. And in truth they were. From a cash income of $1,500 in 1920 Farmer "A" paid $75 in taxes. From a cash income of $600 in 1930, he paid approximately the same.

More important by far in producing the farm crisis, however, was the burden of debt under which the agricultural community was laboring.

This burden, of course, fell unequally. There were large sections of the country where the farms were subject to no mortgages whatsoever. Upon such farms the burden of debt was, of course, inconsequential.

The fact remained, however, that farm after farm throughout the United States was covered by a mortgage, and that these mortgages totaled in the aggregate $8,500,000,000.

The further fact remained that, due to no sloth on their part, due to no fault of their own in so far as they could see, many of these farmers had already lost the land in which their life savings were invested. Thousands upon thousands of others stood upon the verge of doing so.

Owing to a cycle of economic forces over which the American farmer individually had no control, prices and values had so fallen that the charges for interest and amortization which in 1920 took only a reasonable part of his income, took more than twice the original proportion in 1930. Farmer "A," who in 1920 found no difficulty in meeting a $300 interest charge upon his mortgage and little if any embarrassment in reducing the mortgage $500 annually from his cash income of $1,500, in 1930 found it impossible to do so. And Farmer "A" was typical of a large segment of the agricultural community.

These, then, were the factors which had contributed to the farmer's dire distress—overproduction, loss of foreign markets, diminution of demand in the domestic market, and excessive fixed operating charges. These were the problems which the administration must solve if it was to rescue the farmer from his sorry plight.

CHAPTER TEN

INTERNATIONALISM vs. NATIONALISM

Two schools of thought battling to dominate the incoming administration, two groups of advisers struggling for power—this is the picture of almost every new administration. It is perfectly accurate as a description of the political scene in Washington in the year 1933. And on no question, except perhaps that of the currency, has the division of opinion been more clear cut than on the question of agriculture.

Representative of the old-line politicians stood Cordell Hull and Carter Glass, repeating over and over again the familiar arguments of the past. On the other hand, Henry A. Wallace and Rexford G. Tugwell, respectively Secretary and Assistant Secretary of Agriculture, represented the basic philosophies of the New Deal. Both schools agreed as to the causes of the farmer's distress—overproduction, the loss of foreign markets, diminution of demand in the domestic market, and excessively high fixed charges.

The chief item on the agenda of the old-line Democrats was and still is tariff reduction—reciprocal tariff reductions of 5, 10 or 20 per cent, as the exigencies of international bargaining may dictate. This in their opinion would accomplish two things. First, it would introduce into many aspects of American industry an element of competition which, for a long time, has been lacking, since, despite the anti-trust laws, large sections of American industry have been semi-monopolistic in organization. Second, this European competition would force a lowering of prices on the part of the industrialist to a point more nearly commensurate with the level of the price of agricultural commodities. In other words, both agriculture and industry would be selling in a world market at a world price. No longer would the farmer be forced to sell in a free-trade market and to buy in a protected one.

Such a policy, its proponents admit, would undoubtedly cause considerable temporary hardship. It might indeed throw many industries into bankruptcy and force a reorganization of their capital structure. It would, nevertheless, as they see it, establish the basis for a real and lasting recovery. The mere fall in industrial prices would enable the American farmer, even with the cash income of 1932, to order larger and larger consignments of goods. It would, moreover, facilitate the exchange of goods throughout the entire world, and in so doing restore once more an era of business activity. This era of business activity would, in and of itself, do much to increase the demand for farm produce both at home and abroad, with a larger and larger cash income for the farmer. With an increasing demand, agricultural prices would once again begin to rise and the equilibrium between the agricultural and industrial portions of America would be restored. More than that, it would restore world prosperity, without which, in the opinion of the internationalists, the return of national prosperity was exceedingly dubious, if not impossible.

To the nationalist this line of reasoning with regard to our agricultural difficulties was by no means convincing. Two problems remained unsolved by it: first, the problem of overproduction; second, the problem created by the tremendous burden of debt under which the farmer was laboring.

As the nationalist saw it, the internationalist assumed that the lowering of tariff barriers would create, for agricultural produce, a demand of such a character as to absorb not alone the output of the American farmer, but of the entire world. This assumption, the nationalists believed, simply failed to take into consideration the potentially expanding character of farm production. As they saw it, if agriculture was left to itself in the future as it had been in the past, the development of still more effective farm machinery, a wider and wider use of scientific methods of agriculture, and a bringing of a larger and still larger portion of the earth's surface under cultivation would once again, and very shortly, re-create the very situation which had contributed so largely to the débâcle. And if this analysis was correct, agricultural prices, although they might rise for a few months or a year, would once again start plunging downward, leaving the farmer with just exactly as heavy a burden of debt in relation to his income as he had when the policy was inaugurated. In other words, from the point of view of the nationalists, internationalism would save nothing.

One should perhaps call attention to the fact that there were and are two wings of the nationalist group: first, the ultra-nationalists who desire the development of some degree of planned economy—of a concert of interests within America—without any reference whatsoever, save where necessity compels, to the international community; second, the intra-nationalists, who, although they believe that the fundamental necessity is the development of a balanced economy within our own borders, concede not only the need but the desirability of working out, through a series of trade agreements with other nations, something approximating a world concert of interests—a world economy.

To the nationalists, of whichever wing, the first step in the attack upon the problem of agriculture was the curtailment of agricultural production. Only thus, they believed, would it be possible to raise agricultural prices to a level at which the farming community would receive its due share of the national income.

The appointment of Henry A. Wallace as Secretary of Agriculture and of Rexford G. Tugwell as Assistant Secretary of Agriculture pretty definitely indicated the direction in which the tide of battle was flowing. The opening gun of the administration's legislative program—the Agricultural Adjustment Act—proved conclusively that the nationalists had won the day.

The avowed purpose of the Agricultural Adjustment Act was "to bring into closer harmony the abnormally low prices of agricultural commodities and other prices, and to do so with a minimum price rise to the consumer." The price relationship the Roosevelt administration sought to establish was the one that had existed between August, 1909, and July, 1914, in the case of all commodities except tobacco, and, in the case of the latter commodity the relationship that existed between August, 1919, and July, 1929. To this end the Secretary of Agriculture was empowered to enter into agreements with the farmers whereby, in return for a government subsidy, they, the producers of wheat, cotton, corn, hogs, milk and milk products, would not only agree to reduce the number of acres planted, but would also agree to a reduction in their livestock holdings and would consent to follow such other suggestions as the Secretary of Agriculture might initiate to effect reductions in the production of these commodities for the market.

Under the terms of this Act the cotton-producers who would agree to reduce their acreage 30 per cent were given a subsidy of from seven dollars to twenty dollars per acre, depending on the fertility of the land involved, or—"lesser cash benefits and an option on cotton held by the Secretary of Agriculture." Of this last, more anon. The wheat farmer who agreed to reduce his acreage for 1934 and 1935 by not less than 20 per cent has received a subsidy of twenty-eight cents a bushel on the anticipated balance of his crop. This balance incidentally is calculated as 80 per cent of his average crop for the preceding five years. In other words, the American farmer was to be subsidized as an inducement to reduce his output.

The money with which the administration plans to pay these subsidies is to come from a processing or manufacturing tax "levied upon the first domestic processing of the basic commodity concerned." Thus the wheat subsidy is to come from a tax levied upon the miller; the cotton subsidy from the cotton manufacturer, and so on. The rate of the tax is to equal the difference between the present market value and the price level the administration is seeking to establish—except where in the opinion of the Secretary of Agriculture the imposition of such a tax would cause a radical falling off in the demand for the commodity. In fact, of course, as the law anticipates, the processor or manufacturer will pass the burden of the tax on to the ultimate consumer in the form of increased prices. Indeed, so common was the belief that the middle man might use the tax thus imposed as an excuse for profiteering, that a provision was written into the law designed to stop any such attempt.

One unique feature of the Act remains to be discussed —cotton options.

The Federal Farm Board and several other agencies of the Federal government had in their possession enormous cotton holdings and also large equities in future crops. These they were directed to sell to the Secretary of Agriculture at a price not to exceed the existing market price. He, in turn, was to offer to the cotton-planters options on this cotton at the average price he had paid for it, in amounts not in excess of the amount of cotton reduction agreed upon by each cotton-planter—provided in each case that the acreage was reduced by at least 30 per cent. These options might be exercised any time up to January 1, 1934. In no case did the cotton-planter assume any financial liability. Hence, should prices fall, he simply would not exercise his option; should they rise he would sell the cotton and pocket the profit, as in fact he did. An appropriation of $100,000,000 was made from the general funds to cover the expenses incidental to the administration of the act.

These, then, in broad outline, were the essential features of the Act.

Its passage marked a decisive victory of the nationalistic school of thought over the internationalists. It assumes the continued existence of high tariff walls. And behind those tariff walls it is attempting to redistribute wealth between farming and urban classes through a system of subsidies to the farmers, and through the curtailment of farm production to a point where the law of supply and demand within the domestic market will restore the balance of income between agriculture and industry which existed from 1909 to 1914.

CHAPTER ELEVEN

AGRICULTURAL ADJUSTMENT

ON MARCH 4, 1933, when the new administration took office, wheat was selling at 68⅜ cents a bushel, cotton at 6-35/100 cents a pound, beef at 5½ cents a pound, and hogs at 7¼ cents a pound in the New York market. Agricultural prices continued to drop.

How long any individual farmer could hold out depended in large measure upon his financial status. If he owned his property free and clear, he could probably weather the storm. Even then, in many cases, tremendous capital sacrifices would have to be made. Barns in need of reroofing would have to wait another year. Fields in need of fertilizer would have to go without it. Trees in need of spraying would have to go unsprayed. Farm machinery, broken and worn, would have to be crudely patched or laid aside. Personal expenditures would have to be radically curtailed. This was the situation on a thousand and one moderate-sized farms scattered throughout the country.

If there was a mortgage on the farm the situation was infinitely worse. Interest and amortization charges had to be met. In many cases this simply could not be done. Foreclosures, sheriff's sales, evictions followed one after another. One more fatality of the depression was recorded. Another rugged individualist was added to the ranks of the unemployed. In other cases, the carrying charges were met, but frequently at the cost of such deterioration in farm buildings and equipment as to make the future look gloomy indeed.

As we have already observed the Agricultural Adjustment Act was passed on May 12, 1933, and the Agricultural Adjustment Administration was whipped into shape shortly thereafter. A National Administrator, a Co-administrator, a General Counsel, were appointed. A Production Division, Finance Division, Processing and Marketing Division, Planning Division and Publicity Division, were established. (A later reorganization, it might be stated parenthetically, consolidated the Production Division and the Processing and Marketing Division into a Commodities Division. Similarly, experience proved that the major part of the work of the Consumers' Counsel could be consolidated with that of the Publicity Division.) The county agents of the Department of Agriculture's Extension Service were to constitute the shock troops of the entire organization. Thus, the first division of the farm relief expedition got under way.

The attack on overproduction, one of the most powerful of all the deflationary forces, began. The cotton section went into action first. The cotton-producers who would agree to a 30-per-cent reduction in their acreage were given a subsidy of from seven to twenty dollars per acre, depending on the fertility of the soil, or lesser cash benefits and an option on cotton held by the Secretary of Agriculture. Under this stimulus more than 10,000,000 acres of ripening cotton plants were plowed under. Although the crop actually harvested exceeded all estimates, the experts of the Department of Agriculture calculate that at least 4,000,000 bales of cotton were eliminated from the market and the world supply of American cotton was reduced from 26,000,000 bales to 24,800,000.

In return for this reduction in their acreage, the cotton-planters have already received some $182,000,000 in subsidies and some $48,000,000 in profits from the cotton options they exercised. Moreover, through the Commodity Credit Corporation, a subsidiary division of the Department of Agriculture, arrangements were made whereby cotton-planters agreeing to participate in the 1934 acreage reduction campaign might borrow against the cotton still in their possession, at the rate of ten cents a pound. An interest rate of 4 per cent was and is charged against these loans. In this connection, incidentally, a "cotton pool" for the orderly marketing of this cotton was established. As a result of the cotton campaign the official estimates of the Crop Reporting Board of the Department of Agriculture indicate that the total income received by the South for the cotton crop of 1933, including subsidies, was more than twice that received from the crop in 1932—$857,248,000 as over against $425,488,000.

These figures are, perhaps, even more significant when it is realized that had the cotton campaign not taken place the enormous carry-over of American cotton would, in all probability, have driven the price of cotton down to five cents a pound. Had this taken place the sum total income of the cotton planters might easily have fallen well below $400,000,000.

As a result of the activities of the Agricultural Adjustment Administration the cotton South is undoubtedly in better shape today than it has been for months. Recent reports from the region, it is said, indicate that mail-order houses have had their orders almost doubled. The replacement demand for farm machinery has increased 60 per cent and retail trade is up generally.

Plans for the further reduction of the cotton acreage

in 1934 have already been consummated. As a result contracts have already been signed taking approximately 15,000,000 acres of cotton land out of cotton production. It was hoped thus to reduce the tremendous carry-over of American cotton and to restore once again a more normal relationship between supply and demand.

The passage of the Bankhead Cotton Control Act on April 21, 1934, however necessitated a change in plans. Declaring it to be the policy of Congress to promote the orderly marketing of cotton in interstate and foreign commerce, to enable the cotton-producers to stabilize their markets against undue and excessive fluctuation and to balance production more effectively, the Act levied a tax of 50 per cent of the average central market price per pound of lint cotton, upon cotton in excess of 10,000,000 bales which might be ginned from the crop year 1934-35. The minimum tax to be levied was placed at five cents per pound. Allotments of the amount of cotton which may be raised tax free have been allocated among the different states in proportion to their previous cotton production. No state that has produced as much as 250,000 bales of cotton in any one of the preceding five years, however, has received an allotment of less than 200,000 bales. These state allotments are to be prorated among the various counties, and then among the various cotton-producers.

Although the operation of the Bankhead Act is limited to the crop year of 1934-35, it may, with the approval of two-thirds of those interested in cotton production, be extended another year by Presidential proclamation.[1]

[1] For the purpose of relieving the cotton-producers of the necessity of turning to the money-lenders for aid during the planting season incidentally, a portion of the cotton benefits totaling $50,000,000 was

Equally swift and effective was the action which was taken for the relief of the tobacco-growers. Agreements were entered into with over 95 per cent of the tobacco-growers of North Carolina, South Carolina, Virginia, Georgia, and Florida whereby the tobacco crop for 1934 was cut 30 per cent. By virtue of these arrangements it was possible to negotiate an agreement with the tobacco manufacturers whereby they agreed to purchase some 250,000,000 pounds of tobacco—an amount equal to their last year's consumption—at seventeen cents a pound. A limited number of adjustment payments were made in the case of farmers who had already disposed of their crops.

The final result of these negotiations was that the tobacco-growers of the states mentioned received some $120,000,000 for the 1933 crop in contrast with $43,000,000 for that of 1932, and $56,000,000 for that of 1930.

The plan for 1934 is to reduce the total production of tobacco in the United States to 1,000,000,000 pounds in connection with which approximately $40,000,000 in cash benefits will be distributed to the tobacco farmers. Such a reduction should, with the cooperation of the tobacco farmers, increase their income over last year by a full $100,000,000.

A variety of conditions has necessitated a diversity of treatment of the tobacco-growers in different sections of the country. Limitations of space make it impossible to go in detail into the many complicated variations of contract.

The 1933 wheat crop had already been planted when the Agricultural Adjustment Act was passed. The indi-

---

paid them at the time of the signing of the contract. The major part of the balance is to be paid in August and September, the remainder in December.

cations of a light crop made unnecessary the drastic action which had been taken in the case of cotton. Plans for 1934 and 1935, however, were formulated. Contracts were drawn up whereby the signers agreed to reduce their wheat acreage 15 per cent in 1934 and to make a similar reduction at the direction of the Department of Agriculture in 1935. At no time, however, was this reduction to exceed 20 per cent.[2]

As a result of the activities of the wheat section of the Agricultural Adjustment Administration some 550,000 wheat-growers, constituting approximately 80 per cent of all those engaged in the production of wheat, agreed to curtail their production, thus taking some 8,000,000 acres of wheat off the market. Under these agreements something more than $100,000,000 has been or will be paid to the wheat farmers by the way of subsidies. These subsidies, as we have already indicated, are calculated at twenty-eight cents a bushel on the anticipated balance of the crop. This balance is calculated as the average of the preceding five years' production.

At the time the plan was put into effect it was estimated by the officials of the Department of Agriculture that it would reduce the carry-over of American wheat from 389,000,000 bushels as of July 1, 1933, to 300,000,000 bushels as of July 1, 1934, and would increase the income of the wheat farmers by some $200,000,000. As these estimates were made, needless to say, before the drought had occurred in the wheat regions, the reduction in the wheat

2 This national wheat program, incidentally, was part and parcel of an international agreement on the basis of which the other principal wheat nations of the world are planning to reduce their acreage similarly. In view of the crop estimates already available, however, it seems very improbable that this attempt to work out an international solution of the problem of overproduction of wheat will meet with a great degree of success.

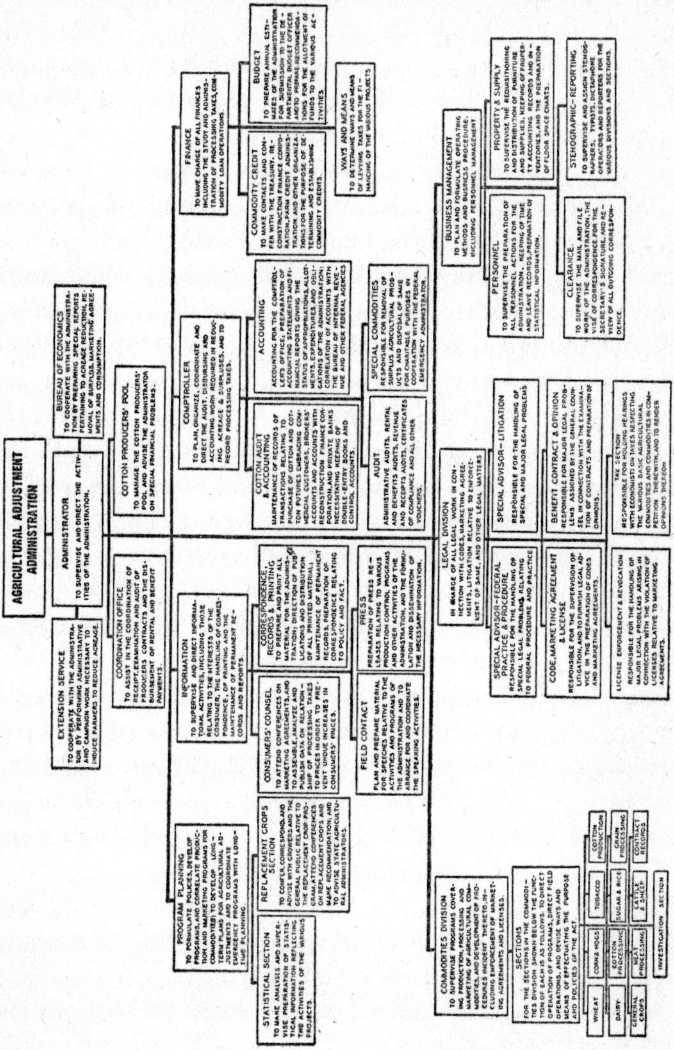
AGRICULTURAL ADJUSTMENT ADMINISTRATION
EXTENSION SERVICE
ADMINISTRATOR
BUREAU OF ECONOMICS
COORDINATION OFFICE
COTTON PRODUCERS' POOL
PROGRAM PLANNING
INFORMATION
COMPTROLLER
FINANCE
STATISTICAL SECTION
REPLACEMENT CROPS SECTION
CONSUMERS' COUNSEL
CORRESPONDENCE, RECORDS & PRINTING
COTTON AUDIT & ACCOUNTING
ACCOUNTING
COMMODITY CREDIT
BUDGET
WAYS AND MEANS
FIELD CONTACT
PRESS
AUDIT
SPECIAL COMMODITIES
COMMODITIES DIVISION
SECTIONS
WHEAT
CORN & HOGS
TOBACCO
COTTON PRODUCTION
DAIRY
COTTON PROCESSING
SUGAR & RICE
GRAIN PROCESSING
GENERAL CROPS
MEAT PROCESSING
CATTLE & SHEEP
CONTRACT RECORDS
INVESTIGATION SECTION
LEGAL DIVISION
SPECIAL ADVISOR—FEDERAL PRACTICE & PROCEDURE
SPECIAL ADVISOR—LITIGATION
CODE, MARKETING AGREEMENT & LICENSE
BENEFIT CONTRACT & OPINION
LICENSE ENFORCEMENT & REVOCATION
TAX SECTION
BUSINESS MANAGEMENT
PERSONNEL
PROPERTY & SUPPLY
CLEARANCE
STENOGRAPHIC—REPORTING

carry-over will be much more radical than was anticipated.

Control of the production of corn and hogs is, perhaps, one of the most difficult problems the Agricultural Adjustment Administration has had to handle.

During the summer of 1933 an attempt was made to curtail the overproduction of pork through a pig-sow campaign. During these months a premium was offered on all pigs weighing less than 100 pounds which were brought to market for slaughter. Approximately 6,000,000 little pigs, which in the normal course of events might have grown to 500 or 600 pounds of pork, were taken off the market. An attempt was made to further curtail pork production by the killing of 1,000,000 sows. Despite the offer of a bonus of four dollars a head above the market price, only 220,000 sows were presented for slaughter. Some of this pork went into inedible grease, some into fertilizer tankage, and some into pork for relief purposes. In any event, it was taken off the market. Some 300,000,000 pounds of pork were purchased for relief purposes during the winter, and because of the anticipated necessity for further relief in the winter of 1934-35 orders have been placed for the purchase of some 2,250,000 additional pigs early in May. Thus, though the campaign was by no means as effective as its sponsors had hoped, it probably did, nevertheless, strengthen the hog market.

The campaign for the reduction of the corn yield and the still further reduction of hog production is already under way. Corn farmers who have agreed to withhold 20 per cent of their corn land from production will be paid thirty cents a bushel for the corn they have agreed not to produce. Thus Farmer "A," who has reduced his corn acreage from one hundred to eighty acres, and who in the past has grown forty bushels to the acre, will be paid at the rate of twelve dollars an acre, a sum of $240, for allowing his land to lie idle. Checks for two-thirds of the benefit payments have already been mailed. The remainder is to be mailed this fall. It was hoped in this manner to reduce the total corn production throughout the country by 500,000,000 bushels.

Similarly, the hog-producer who has agreed to reduce his output 25 per cent will receive a bonus of five dollars a head on the remaining 75 per cent of his production. In fact, two-fifths of this subsidy has already reached him. The second payment of one dollar per head will be made on or about September 1, 1934, "upon certification by the county association that the producer has, in fact, reduced the number of litters farrowed" by the 25 per cent agreed upon. The third and final payment of two dollars per head may be expected about February 1, 1935, "upon certification by the county association that the number of hogs farrowed was 25 per cent under the average number farrowed and marketed" in the years immediately preceding.

In addition, farmers who are participating in the crop-reduction program may obtain loans from the new Commodity Credit Corporation on the security of corn still in their possession up to the grand total of $150,000,000 at an interest rate of 4 per cent. In the making of such loans the corn so pledged is evaluated at from forty-five to fifty cents a bushel, depending upon the grade of corn.

Of the 1,500,000 corn-hog producers in the country some 1,200,000 have already signed contracts. At this writing some $200,000,000 in benefit checks has been mailed to the corn farmers; approximately $150,000,000 more will follow.

As a consequence of the drought, four modifications have had to be made in the plans of the Agricultural Adjustment Administration. It has been necessary in the first place to speed up the payment of the adjustment benefits. In the second place, the original contracts with both the wheat and corn farmers have had to be radically modified so as both to release the farmers from the necessity of planting wheat and corn in the manner called for by the contracts and to permit the planting of forage crops in a manner, and to an extent, previously prohibited. In the third place a plan of purchasing and transporting cattle from the drought areas has had to be worked out, since to allow nature to take its course would mean both the glut of the cattle market because of the forced sale of herds which could not be carried through the summer, and a tremendous financial loss for the farmers not only in the drought area, but everywhere, by virtue of falling prices. Finally, a reduction in transportation rates from the drought areas seemed desirable. Despite the drought, however, the problem of the Agricultural Adjustment Administration remains unchanged,—that is, the problem of balancing production and consumption through the curtailment of production.

The drought has emphasized, nevertheless, the danger of cutting production too radically. The Secretary of Agriculture has, therefore, raised the question of the desirability of carrying over from year to year a tremendous supply of agricultural produce for emergency purposes, ear-marked in such a way as permanently to keep it off the market. That the total elimination of the agricultural surpluses which have hitherto been depressing the market will cause a radical alteration in the plans of the Agricultural Adjustment Administration can be taken for granted.

The progress which the Agricultural Adjustment Administration has thus far made in the field of dairying is, perhaps, the least satisfactory of all its endeavors. As an emergency measure the Dairy Marketing Corporation was set up, and from time to time has purchased butter for distribution through the Federal Surplus Relief Corporation. A marketing agreement by which the manufacturers of evaporated milk have agreed to pay the farmer a minimum price for their milk has likewise been consummated. Although, through the technique of marketing agreements and licensing, certain market practices unfair to the farmers have been eliminated, a fundamental reorganization of the industry has not in any measure been attained—nor, for that matter one might add, even been seriously attempted.

Equally unsatisfactory has been the progress in the fields of beef production, poultry, and eggs. In connection with fruits and vegetables likewise, although various and sundry market agreements have been entered into, nothing fundamental has been accomplished.

At the last session of the seventy-third Congress, however, seven additional basic commodities—beef, dairy cattle, peanuts, rice, barley, flax, grain sorghums, and sugar—were added to those already included within the compass of the Act. Plans are now being formulated in connection with each of these commodities to bring the supply into better balance with the demand but down to date the activities of the Agricultural Adjustment Administration have not progressed far enough in this regard to warrant comment.[3]

Despite all these efforts which have been made the forces of deflation in the field of agriculture have not, it is clear, been utterly routed. It is, nevertheless, equally evident that some progress has been made. Enormous sums have been added to the farm income by way of subsidies; the cotton farmers have received or will receive $150,000,000; the wheat farmers, $110,000,000; the tobacco-planters, approximately $19,000,000; the corn and hog farmers, $350,000,000; a grand total of $600,000,000 even when due allowance is made for inaccuracies in estimates. Certain agricultural commodities, moreover, are selling at distinctly higher prices. Indeed, it is estimated that the total cash income of the agricultural regions of the United States was approximately 40 per cent higher during the year which terminated May 1, 1934 than it had been in the year preceding.

To assert that this rise in agricultural prices is wholly attributable to the work of the Agricultural Adjustment Administration would be obviously untrue. It is probable, however, that a substantial portion of this increase may justifiably be attributed to the activities of that organization. That the drought has seriously affected the welfare of large sections of the agricultural community is self-evident. That the consequences of the drought would have been even more serious in the regions affected

[3] Mention should be made, perhaps, of the activities of the Federal Surplus Relief Corporation which was organized for the double purpose of removing agricultural surpluses from the commodity markets and providing food for the destitute. Under its auspices some thirty million dollars have been expended, which have without question contributed somewhat to relieving the acuteness of the immediate situation both among the farmers and among the unemployed.

except for the activities of the Agricultural Adjustment Administration needs no substantiation.

Whether it is possible, however, to have prosperity without plenty, whether a stimulation of consumption rather than the curtailment of production would not have been more desirable in the long run, whether the redirection of agricultural energies might not have been a more statesmanlike policy—are questions only time can answer. No less important is the question whether as a long-time policy the Agricultural Adjustment Act is possible of administration. Once again—only time will tell.

CHAPTER TWELVE

THE FARMER'S MARKETS

THE efforts of the administration to meet the problems of agriculture have by no means been confined to an attack on overproduction. Equally significant has been the attempt to restore the farmer's former markets. For the most part this has been a flanking operation rather than a frontal attack.

Although the primary motive for the repeal of prohibition was not in any sense the desirc to restore the farmers' domestic market, nevertheless such restoration may well be its effect. Unless the drinking habits of the American people have radically changed since the days which preceded the "noble experiment," the market for farm produce which was lost upon the enactment of prohibition may again be restored. Estimates of the market which was lost vary considerably. The most accurate seems to be that of Ostrolenk, to which reference has already been made. He calculates that the passage of prohibition reduced the consumption of barley by some 65,000,000 bushels, of corn by some 33,000,000 bushels, and of hops by some 35,000,000 bushels. Whether the recapture of this market for the grain farmers will mean a diminution of the market for other agricultural produce is a question impossible of definitive answer. A considerable body of opinion, however, inclines to the belief that the use of alcoholic beverages will increase rather than diminish the consumption of foodstuffs generally.

Similarly, the increases in relief appropriations and the establishment of the Civil Works Administration, although primarily designed as a solution of the relief problem, were and are not without a direct relation to the domestic market for agricultural produce.

The average relief dole for a family of five in the City of New York during the month of August, 1932, was less than twenty-four dollars a month for food, clothing, gas, electricity, medicine, and shelter. Had this entire sum been allotted for food, it would still have averaged less than eighty cents a day, or twenty-six and two-thirds cents a meal for a family of five. And New York was rather generous in her distribution of relief! It is therefore probably safe to assert that during the major part of the depression a large section of the unemployed have actually had insufficient food.

It is probable that a considerable proportion of the money poured out by the government for relief purposes, whether through direct relief, newly voted old-age pensions, or the Civil Works Administration, was used and is being used for the purchase of foodstuffs and has, in consequence, constituted another step in the restoration of the domestic market for farm produce. The public-works program has undoubtedly functioned in a similar fashion. Designed though it was to stimulate once again employment in the heavy industries, it undoubtedly has contributed to the further restoration of the normal demand for foodstuffs.

A similar comment might be made upon the National Industrial Recovery Administration, designed, in part at least, to increase the purchasing power of the masses. For it seems almost axiomatic that, all other things remaining the same, the restoration of the purchasing power of the masses will, in and of itself, go a long way toward the restoration of a normal demand for farm produce in the domestic markets. Indeed, one might almost sustain the thesis that if urban purchasing power were redistributed in such a way that a larger share of it went to the masses instead of the classes the sum total demand for farm produce would be increased.

Exceedingly vital, if not equally important with the restoration of the home market for farm produce, is the regaining of our former foreign markets. To this end four lines of attack have been formulated. The first, the extension of credit abroad; the second, the depreciation of the American dollar; the third, the policy of dumping goods abroad below the domestic price; and the fourth, the negotiation of reciprocal tariffs.

In view of the unfortunate experience of the country with the practice of lending money abroad during the Coolidge and Hoover administrations, one might expect to find considerable hesitation in Washington over the further continuance of such a policy. Nevertheless, the fact is that the Roosevelt administration has already extended a credit of some $50,000,000 to the Chinese government for the purchase of American cotton. And there is some evidence that a similar policy is contemplated with regard to Russia. The problem, as one wing of the Roosevelt administration analyzes it, is one of selection. The mistake of the Coolidge and Hoover administrations in permitting credit to be extended abroad was that the loans were made to industrial and agricultural countries which by the nature of their social and economic organization were either active or potential competitors of the United States in the pursuit of world trade. The credit we extended was merely used to render their industrial and commercial machinery more effective in their competition with us.

As these analysts see it, this is not the case with either China or Russia. In each of these countries, they believe, there exists a social system which will enable the masses to absorb an ever-increasing output for some years to come. In other words, the domestic market in both China and Russia is so huge that this wing of the administration believes it will be decades before either country will become a dangerous competitor for world trade. Hence, it would appear, loans may be extended to them without the danger of an aftermath such as followed the extension of credit to the industrial nations of Europe.

Just what we are to receive in return for these loans has not as yet been made entirely clear. In this connection, incidentally, two Import-Export banks have been established.

A second line of action designed to stimulate our exports, agricultural produce included, has, as already indicated, been the depreciation of the American dollar. On March 14, 1933, the first day foreign exchange rates were published after the banking crisis, it was possible to exchange the pound for $3.42; the franc for 3.92 cents; the lira for 5.12 cents; the mark for 23.86 cents; the yen for 21.94 cents; the rupee for 25.69 cents; the Hongkong dollar for 23.94 cents; and the Shanghai dollar for 29.94 cents.

Today, it is possible to exchange the pound for $5.09; the franc for 6.67 cents; the lira for 8.69 cents; the mark for 39.60 cents; the yen for 30.18 cents; the rupee for 38.37 cents; the Hongkong dollar for 39.12 cents; and the Shanghai dollar for 35.50 cents.

As I indicated in a preceding chapter, all other things

remaining the same, the depreciation of the American dollar in terms of foreign currencies should lead to the export of a greater and greater volume of American produce, agricultural and industrial alike. Tariff barriers are thus over-ridden, and railroad differentials overcome. In so far as this has not taken place, it may be taken for granted that counterbalancing factors have entered the situation.

The great danger of embarking on such a policy was, the possibility of precipitating a trade war. That the administration has recognized this possibility is evidenced by the fact that for the past several months there has been a striking cessation of radical monetary manipulation. Also there has seemingly been an attempt to stabilize the dollar at a more or less fixed ratio with the other currencies of the world—a ratio, however, which has corrected somewhat the disadvantages under which the American exporter had previously been suffering.

A third policy which has been followed by the administration in its endeavor to recover the farmer's former export markets is that of "dumping." The North Pacific Export Association was formed under a marketing agreement with producers, millers, and exporters in Washington, Oregon, and Northern Idaho. Its purpose was the elimination of the price-depressing surplus of the Northwestern States through the export to the Orient or elsewhere of wheat and flour purchased at the domestic price but sold at the world prices. The difference, which has averaged between twenty-one and twenty-three cents a bushel is to be met from processing taxes. Down to date some 25,758,000 bushels of wheat have been purchased and 25,431,000 exported. And it is planned to dump between thirty and thirty-five million bushels abroad before the end of the year.

Equally significant, however, in the effort to restore the farmer's former foreign markets, is a fourth line of endeavor. It was forecast by the establishment within the Department of State of a division the primary purpose of which was the negotiation of trade agreements with Europe whereby American agricultural produce would be allowed access to European markets in return for the admission of certain alcoholic beverages to the American market. The passage of the Reciprocal Tariff Act of June 12, 1934, constituted a second step in the development of this policy. Under its provision the President is authorized for a period of three years to negotiate trade agreements with foreign governments without the traditional advice and consent of the Senate and by proclamation to raise and lower tariff rates by not more than 50 per cent. These provisions introduce a measure of flexibility hitherto impossible under American tariff laws. It may well be that in this line of endeavor will be found the real stimulus to our export trade.

To what extent the consequences of the drought will necessitate a modification of these policies, remains to be seen.

Whether a creditor nation can, over a long period of time, maintain a favorable balance of trade, is, to put it mildly, highly controversial.

CHAPTER THIRTEEN

MORTGAGE RELIEF

COMMENDABLE though the Agricultural Adjustment Act and the various and sundry measures designed to restore the farmer's markets might be, they were of little or no value to the farmer about to be dispossessed. They were all, in a sense, long-time projects.

During the five years immediately preceding March 15, 1932, approximately 10 per cent of the farms of the country had been sold at public auction, and the number was rapidly increasing. Was the administration to stand pat until the consequences of long-time agricultural planning became apparent, or was further action to be taken?

A direct attack upon the problem of farm credit seemed imperative.

A series of amendments to the Federal Farm Loan Act were whipped into shape; the Federal Farm Credit Act was drafted. Thus the administration's attack upon the mortgage situation got under way. The Federal Land Banks, which had been established in 1916, were authorized to issue bonds up to a total of $2,000,000,000. These bonds were to be used for the making of new loans or the refinancing of old ones. They were to bear interest at 4 per cent, and the interest was to be fully and unconditionally guaranteed by the Federal government. No loan to be made through the medium of the Federal Land Banks, however, was to exceed 50 per cent of the normal value of the land pledged as security, except that an additional loan might be made on the basis of any permanent improvements up to 20 per cent of the value of such improvements.

To encourage the Federal Land Banks to renew such loans as might already be outstanding, the Secretary of the Treasury was directed to subscribe to the paid-in surplus of the land banks an amount equal to any extensions or deferments.

The interest rate on any mortgage which might be purchased from a joint-stock land bank in the course of its liquidation was to be reduced to 4½ per cent. Any loss of income which might thus accrue to any Federal Land Bank was to be made up from the public treasury.[1] If a borrower had not otherwise defaulted, all compulsory amortization payments were to be suspended for a period of five years. Where there were no national farm loan associations, the Federal Land Banks were empowered to make loans to the farmers directly.

Finally, the Reconstruction Finance Corporation was directed to place at the disposal of the Farm Loan Commissioner a fund of $200,000,000 from which he was empowered to extend loans to farmers on first or second mortgages. This money might be used to refinance any previously acquired indebtedness, to redeem or repurchase any land which had been foreclosed after July 1, 1931, or it might be used for working capital. In no case, however, was the sum total indebtedness of any farmer to whom such an emergency loan was made to exceed 75 per cent of the normal value of his property.

[1] Provision was made for the orderly liquidation of the joint-stock land banks, which are consequently in the process of passing out of the agricultural credit picture.

Such, in broad outline, was the first of the relief measures aimed at the alleviation of the tremendous burden of debts under which the farmer labored.

The bulk of the money which was to be used for the relief of the harassed farmers, be it noted, was to come not from the public treasury, but from the investing public. A nice problem in public policy presented itself in consequence. On what basis was the "normal value" of the land pledged as security for the mortgages to be determined?

"If we are going to operate this system successfully," said William I. Myers, governor of the Farm Credit Administration, "we must maintain the confidence of investors, which means that the loans must be sound. The Farm Credit Administration believes that agriculture needs a complete system of credit and that farmers will be better off if this system provides the opportunity for individual farmers, through organization, to obtain their funds from the investment market. The Federal Land Banks have been and still are obtaining their funds to loan to farmers on the security of farm mortgages from the sale of bonds, secured by those farm mortgages."

Still the question was not answered. On what basis was the normal value of the land pledged as security for the mortgages to be determined? Loans up to 10 per cent of existing values would certainly give the investor ample protection. Loans as high as 50 per cent of the current value would probably be considered satisfactory. Such an ultra-conservative policy of lending mortgage money, however, would have done little or nothing to help the farmer out of his predicament. Possibly with the farmer primarily in mind the Farm Credit Administration reached the decision that all land pledged as security for mortgage loans should be appraised—not on the basis of the depressed values which existed on May 12, 1933, when the Act was passed, but on those during the base period selected by Congress in the Agricultural Adjustment Act, the period from 1909 to 1914.

With this major decision out of the way, the work of building an adequate administrative organization began.

Some slight conception of the magnitude of the task may be obtained from the fact that in the year preceding May 12, 1933, the twelve Federal Land Banks had made exactly 7,208 loans, totaling $27,000,000. In the five and one-half months immediately following the passage of the Act, the Farm Credit Administration was the recipient of 433,037 applications for loans totaling $1,724,363,809. On May 12, 1933, after seventeen years of operation, the Federal Land Banks had outstanding $1,000,000,000 of mortgage loans. Between May 12 and December 1, 1933, the Farm Credit Administration was asked to approve $1,724,363,809 in loans. In other words, in five and a half months the Farm Credit Administration received application for a volume of credit greater than the loans the Federal Land Banks had outstanding after seventeen years of operation. Since then applications have been pouring in at the rate of ten to twelve thousand a week.

Limits of space making it impossible to describe in detail the various problems arising out of the administration of the emergency mortgage-relief program. One of the most staggering problems, perhaps, was that of appraisal. On May 12, 1933, when the Act was passed, all twelve land banks could marshal only 210 appraisers.

The first task of the Farm Credit Administration, consequently, was the training of new appraisers. This took time. For several weeks, moreover, this task took almost the full time of the few trained appraisers who might otherwise have been in the field. A tremendous back-log of applications for loans piled up in the several banks. Indeed, not until the administration had over 4,000 appraisers in the field were they able to appraise the applications as fast as they came in. And not until almost 5,000 were in the field was it possible to make substantial inroads on the pile of applications which had accumulated.

Because of this seemingly inevitable delay a division was created within the Farm Credit Administration to assist distressed borrowers in getting foreclosures stayed until their cases were reached. As a result of this division's activities, some 13,000 foreclosures have thus far been forestalled, and other cases are still being handled at the rate of 400 a day.

To have made loans only up to 50 per cent of even the normal value of the average farm, and to 20 per cent of the value of the permanent improvements thereon would in no way have afforded adequate relief to many a farmer. In recognition of this fact, as we have already observed, Congress placed $200,000,000 at the disposal of the Farm Land Commissioner with which to save, if possible, the marginal farmer. With this money the Farm Loan Commission might extend a further loan against a second mortgage up to 75 per cent of the value of the property involved. "It was not the intention of Congress, however, merely to transfer the burden of debts from the present creditors to the Federal government and leave the farmer so badly in debt he could not work out; and so if the farmer is to borrow from the Commissioner up to 75 per cent of the value of his farm property, it is necessary that he compose his debts within this amount. In other words, this means that if his debts are in excess of this amount, they must be scaled down to 75 per cent."

The question immediately arose as to why a farmer's creditors should forego their just claims? Some creditors were exceedingly critical of the demand. But when it was pointed out to them that 75 per cent of the normal value of a farm property was as much as they could obtain through a foreclosure sale, anyway, they usually saw the light and preferred to take their proportionate share of the cash in settlement, rather than spend their money on foreclosure fees.

In order to assist in the conciliation of debtors and creditors the Farm Credit Administration suggested to the governors of the forty-eight states that they appoint special committees to bring the debtors and creditors together. Following this suggestion, forty-two states have set up such commissions, and some 2,400 counties have established similar bodies. Down to August 5, 1934, adjustments totaling more than $100,000,000 had been made under their auspices.

The recent extension of the Federal guarantee to the principal as well as to the interest of the bonds issued by the Federal Land Banks has enabled the Farm Credit Administration to reduce the interest rate on the bonds offered for sale from 4 per cent to 3 per cent, thus saving the administration a considerable sum of money. In view of the fact that the bonds, so guaranteed, immediately sold at par or slightly above, the Farm Credit Administration very shortly thereafter instituted the procedure of exchanging bonds for mortgages, rather than paying cash, thus expediting the work of the office. In view of the fact that the recipient of the bonds could immediately convert them into cash no administrative difficulties were encountered by virtue of the change of procedure. As a result of these activities, approximately $1,000,000,000 has been loaned to some 400,000 farmers down to date, and in one out of every ten cases, debts have been scaled down approximately 25 per cent.

More important, foreclosures of farm property have practically ceased, and, whether due to relief from the pressure of forced sales or to other factors, the value of rural real estate has been steadily rising.

CHAPTER FOURTEEN

AGRICULTURAL CREDITS

Not satisfied with the mere extension of relief to those farmers who were in distress because of their burden of debts, the administration has attempted to set up a system of agricultural credits which will relieve the agricultural regions generally of their dependence upon the commercial money market. To this end a series of Intermediate Credit Banks, Central and Regional Banks for Cooperatives, Production Credit Corporations and Associations, have been established.

The Intermediate Credit Banks, one should indicate parenthetically, have been in existence for a number of decades. The action of the administration relative to these institutions, consequently, has been a mere modification of their previously existing activities.

A glance at the accompanying chart will reveal the fact that in each of the twelve Federal Land Bank districts there is now a Federal Land Bank, a Bank for Cooperatives, an Intermediate Credit Bank, and a Production Credit Corporation. The Board of Trustees of each of these institutions is identical in personnel. By virtue of this fact it is hoped to attain that coordination between these various institutions which alone makes for efficiency. An advisory committee, made up of the president of each institution together with a general agent of the Farm Credit Administration, will in all probability dictate the policies to be followed.

The Federal Land Banks, as we have already indicated in our previous discussion, are chiefly concerned with long-time investments—mortgages.

The Intermediate Credit Banks, as the name implies, provide credits which fall between the short-time commercial paper to which the Commercial Banks theoretically confine themselves and the mortgages in which the Land Banks deal. The Intermediate Banks make no loans to private individuals, but are instead the discount banks of the various financial institutions dealing in intermediate paper, agricultural cooperatives, live-stock loan companies, production credit corporations, certain state and national banks, etc. These latter institutions extend loans directly to the individual farmer. They may borrow from the Intermediate Credit Bank either on the basis of their own security or on the basis of such agricultural and live-stock paper as the Intermediate Bank deems sound. The amount of credit which can thus be extended in the case of banks is limited to twice their paid-in and unimpaired capital and surplus, and in the case of other agricultural credit institutions to from two to eight times their unimpaired capital.

Incidentally, the discount rate which the Intermediate Credit Bank may charge may not exceed by more than 1 per cent the interest rate of the last series of debentures issued by a given bank. Thus, if an Intermediate Credit Bank has last sold its debentures for 2½ per cent it may establish a discount rate of not more than 3½ per cent. The borrowing institution is limited in its turn in that it may not charge the individual farmer more than 3 per cent in excess of the rate at which it can discount its paper. In ordinary cases the loans extended by the Intermediate Credit Bank will run from six months to a year;

in extraordinary cases they may extend to three years. Thus, like the Federal Reserve, the Intermediate Credit Banks are really bankers' banks.

Equally important in the newly established agricultural credit machinery are the Central and Regional Banks for Cooperatives.

A Central Bank for Cooperatives with a capital of $50,-000,000 has been set up in Washington. And in each of the twelve districts a regional institution with functions very similar to those of the Central Bank has also been established. Although at the moment each of these regional banks has a capital of $5,000,000, this capital may be expanded or contracted by the governor of the Farm Credit Administration as the needs of the district dictate.

Both the Central and the Regional Banks for Cooperatives are authorized to make loans for the same purposes; both are subject to the same limitations. By and large the broad line of demarcation between them seems to be the size of the loan requested. All applications for loans in excess of $300,000 are referred to the Central Bank in Washington, although applications for loans of less than $500,000 are frequently referred back to the regional institutions for final action.

Cooperative associations obtaining loans from either the Central or Regional Banks must own or purchase, at the time a loan is made, an amount of stock in the bank equal to 5 per cent of the loan. Upon repayment of the loan, this stock will be retired at the purchase price, less a pro-rata impairment of the stock if such an impairment has taken place. Should the state laws under which a cooperative has been formed not permit the cooperative to subscribe to stock, the cooperative must, if it desires to borrow from the Cooperative Bank, pay into a guarantee fund a sum equal to the subscription it would otherwise have to make.

Thus a cushion against possible losses has been established.

Loans may be made to cooperatives either for purchasing or merchandising purposes, or for the construction or acquisition of the physical properties necessary to the functioning of the cooperative. No loan, designed for this latter purpose, however, may exceed 60 per cent of the value of the properties to be acquired. In addition to making loans to cooperative associations, the Central Bank may also make such loans to the twelve regional cooperative banks as seem to it wise—under conditions and rules to be laid down by the Cooperative Bank Commissioner.

Incidentally, the interest rate to be charged must conform as closely as practicable to 1 per cent in excess of the discount rate charged by the Intermediate Credit Banks,—in the case of loans designed to expedite the purchasing and merchandising of commodities,—and, in the case of loans intended to make possible the acquisition of physical facilities—to the prevailing rate of interest on land-bank mortgages at the time. After operating expenses, losses, and amounts necessary to offset impairment of capital have been deducted from earnings, the Central Bank for Cooperatives must apply 25 per cent of the balance to the creation and maintenance of a surplus, equal to at least 25 per cent of the capital and guarantee fund. Any balance still remaining may, with the approval of the chairman of the board, be devoted to the payment of dividends, which may at no time, however, amount to more than 7 per cent per annum.

The Board of Directors of the Central Bank, incidentally, is to consist of seven members, the Cooperative Bank Commissioner and six others appointed by the governor of the Farm Credit Administration. The successors of the first three appointed, are to be chosen, one each year, from a panel presented by the borrowers.

The last of the units of the new system of agricultural credits are the twelve Production Credit Corporations, capitalized at $7,500,000 each.

The function of these corporations is the investment of the funds at their disposal in Class A stock of the

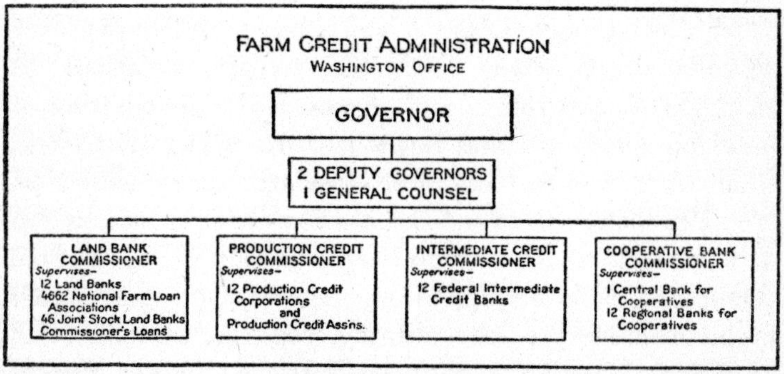

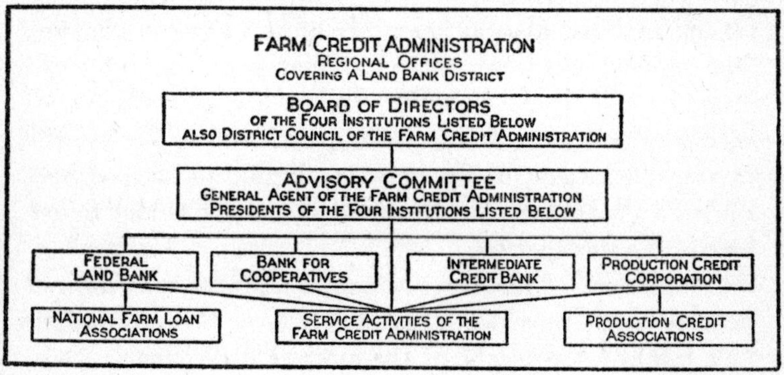

Production Credit Associations which are to be established in their respective districts. The Production Credit Corporations are authorized to purchase stock in each association in their respective districts to an amount sufficient to maintain the Class A stock holdings of the Association equal to 20 per cent of the loans made to the farmers. The funds so obtained are to be invested by each association in high-grade bonds. These are to constitute a back-log which, when presented with the notes of the individual farmers to whom production loans may be extended, will suffice to enable these Production Credit Associations to rediscount their paper at the Federal Intermediate Credit Banks.

Needless to say, Class A stock has a preference over all other assets of the production credit association. It is, however, non-voting and shares in the distribution of dividends only on equal terms with the Class B stock to which all borrowers from these associations must subscribe.

A Production Credit Association may be formed by ten or more farmers desiring to borrow money for production purposes. To be eligible to become part of the production credit machinery of the country, however, the officers of each such association must be approved by the Corporation, and the association itself must receive a charter. The capital stock of these associations falls into two classes, Class A and Class B. Only Class B stock carries voting privileges. It may be purchased only by the farmer borrowers, or by persons eligible to become borrowers. Possession of such stock entitles the holder to one vote in the Association.

At the time of receiving a loan, borrowers are required to have or to purchase Class B stock in the Association to a total of 5 per cent of the amount of the loan. Subscriptions to this stock may be purchased from the proceeds of the loan, however. Normally no single individual will be permitted to borrow more than 20 per cent of the capital and guarantee fund of the Association, although under exceptional circumstances this amount may be increased to 50 per cent of the base thus established. Interest rates on those loans vary. But under no circumstances may they amount to more than 3 per cent in excess of the discount rate of the Intermediate Credit Banks. At the moment, the rate which is being charged is 5 per cent. The duration of the loans will ordinarily be determined by the length of time required to complete the farm operations thus being financed. Usually, however, the notes will not run for more than twelve months.

Although Class B stock once issued cannot be retired, it can be exchanged for Class A stock which can be retired. Indeed, each holder of Class B stock must make such an exchange within two years after repayment of his loan. Dividends on both Class A and Class B stocks are limited to 7 per cent. No dividends may be paid, however, until a guarantee fund equal to 25 per cent of the paid-in capital has been established.

This, briefly, is the system of agricultural credits which has been established. The extent to which it will supplant the commercial banks as instruments of agricultural credits remains to be seen.

Nevertheless, the fact that some 1,600 agricultural cooperatives have been formed and some 658 production credit associations have been chartered is not without its significance. Nor, indeed, can the fact that within a relatively short space of time some $100,000,000 has been loaned through these various and sundry agencies to approximately 100,000 farmers be totally disregarded.

CHAPTER FIFTEEN

FARM BANKRUPTCY

A STILL further line of attack upon the farm problem is embodied in the Frazier-Lemke-Long Farm Bankruptcy Act of 1934. Briefly summarized the Act makes it possible for a farmer who finds himself unable to arrive at a satisfactory settlement with his creditors to file a petition in bankruptcy, with the request that he be permitted to retain possession of his property. Upon the receipt of such an application the court will appoint an appraiser to make a fair and reasonable appraisal of the property, although not necessarily at the market value. From this, the farmer will be allowed to subtract the usual personal exemptions. The balance will be allocated by the court among his various creditors in the form of a lien upon the property. The property, however, is to continue in the possession of the debtor.

Two possibilities of settlement will then be open. At the request of the debtor the trustee may, with the consent of the lien-holders, agree to sell the property to the debtor upon "(a) the payment of 1 per cent interest upon the appraised price within one year from the date of said agreement, (b) the payment of 2½ per cent of the appraised price within two years from the date of said agreement, (c) the payment of an additional 2½ per cent of the appraised price within three years from the date of the agreement, (d) the payment of an additional

5 per cent within five years from the date of agreement, (e) the payment of an additional 5 per cent within five years and (f) the payment of the balance within six years." Interest is to be paid upon the appraised price and unpaid balance at the rate of 1 per cent per annum. All taxes, however, are to be paid by the debtor.

If any creditor should refuse to enter into such an agreement, the court will then stay all proceedings for a period of five years, during which the debtor may remain in possession of the property, provided he pays a reasonable rental to be fixed by the court. At the end of five years, or prior thereto, the debtor may pay into the court the appraised price of the property. Upon the request of any lien-holder, however, a second appraisal of the property may be made at this time. Should this second appraisal place a greater value upon the property than the previous one, the debtor must make up the additional amount. Should the second appraisal be no higher than the first, the court will accept the payment of the original appraisal price and turn over both the property and the title thereto to the debtor, who may then apply for discharge from bankruptcy.

The Farm Bankruptcy Act will undoubtedly prevent the eviction of many a marginal farmer. What it will do to the capital markets for farm mortgages not guaranteed by the Federal government remains to be seen.

INDUSTRY

CHAPTER SIXTEEN

THE NATIONAL RECOVERY ACT

No less acute than the plight of the farmers was the situation in which millions of industrial workers found themselves in March, 1933.

Two courses of action were possible in the field of industry, as there had been in agriculture; the first sponsored by the orthodox, the second by the heterodox economists. The theory of the orthodox economists was that the deflation should be allowed to run its course. Agriculture had already been deflated. It was only necessary, consequently, for industry to be equally deflated, and we should, once again, reach a state of economic equilibrium in which business could thrive and prosper. According to the orthodox ideal the tariff should be repealed, or at least radically lowered (and another two or three million men temporarily thrown out of work) to permit a free play of world economic forces. Vigorous action should be taken by the Attorney-General under the anti-trust laws. The patent laws might have to be amended. Business after business would, of course, go through bankruptcy. Quite probably the savings-banks and insurance companies would have to go also. It might take some six months or a year for the deflation in industry to run its course, but, when it had, we should have attained our desideratum—an economic equilibrium.

Just what would happen to this equilibrium once it

had been attained our orthodox advisers have never indicated.

Unfortunately, the atmosphere of March 4, 1933, was not the atmosphere of the academician's study. Thirteen to fourteen million men were out of work. Thirty to forty million persons were in the families of the nation's unemployed. Cut-throat competition was forcing wages down to starvation levels. Sweatshops were paying $3.50 to $5.00 a week; day labor in certain sections of the country was receiving seventy-five cents to one dollar a day. The stock market was recording disheartening lows. Intellectuals were discussing the end of capitalism. It was an atmosphere in which the most courageous politicians might well hesitate to let the inexorable laws of economics work out the destinies of our economic order. How much farther could the deflationary forces continue their downward course, how much more would the people endure before there would be a social convolution—a revolution? This was the question which was in the back of many a politician's mind, even when it was not upon his tongue.

Rightly or wrongly, the administration reached the conclusion that—whatever might have been the wise policy in 1929—in 1933 the depression could no longer be permitted to work itself out. Action would have to be taken. The deflation would have to be stopped. As part of the general counter-deflationary program then agreed on, the National Industrial Recovery Act was formulated. The essential purpose of the Act is set forth in its first section:

A national emergency productive of widespread unemployment and disorganization of industry, which burdens interstate and foreign commerce, affects the public welfare and undermines the standards of living of the American people, is hereby declared to exist. It is hereby declared to be the policy of Congress to remove obstructions to the free flow of interstate and foreign commerce which tend to diminish the amount thereof; and to provide for the general welfare by promoting the organization of industry for the purpose of cooperative action among trade groups, to induce and maintain united action of labor and management under adequate governmental sanctions and supervision, to eliminate unfair competitive practices, to promote the fullest possible utilization of the present productive capacity of industries, to avoid undue restrictions of production (except as may be temporarily required), to increase the consumption of industrial and agricultural products by increasing purchasing power, to reduce and relieve unemployment, to improve standards of labor, and otherwise to rehabilitate industry and to conserve natural resources.

As the Act has been interpreted by its administrators four major objectives appear to have been paramount: (1) the spreading of work among the unemployed through the elimination of child labor and a reduction of working hours; (2) an increase in the purchasing power of the masses; (3) the stimulation of labor union organization; and (4) the abolition of unfair competition among business men and the introduction of at least a modicum of planning into industry. These objectives were by no means new in American life. The movement for the elimination of child labor had behind it a history of a quarter of a century. While a few die-hards still remain who subscribe to the theory that the labor of children of tender years is socially desirable, their numbers have been constantly diminishing. In consequence, the elimination of child labor through the National Industrial Recovery

Act was in fact the culmination of a quarter-century drive for improved social conditions.

Similarly, the movement for shorter working-hours is no new thing in American politics. Court decision after court decision bears mute testimony to the onward march of the movement. Although there are many who believe in the dignity of human labor, the number of those who now believe a ten- or twelve-hour day either necessary or desirable has practically vanished.

More important than the social philosophy which lies behind the child-labor movement or the campaign for a reduction of the working-day, in securing the introduction of these provisions into the recovery program was the simple fact that the elimination of child labor and a reduction of the working-day would automatically increase the amount of employment available for adult workers, and in so doing would thus restore to employment tens of thousands of adult workers who were at the moment on the relief rolls. In this fashion, also, it was reasoned that the sum total purchasing power of the nation would be increased, for it was understood that there would be no decrease in wages proportionate to the decrease in the number of working-hours.

The movement for a minimum-wage law has behind it likewise an ancient and honorable history. The movement was, for the most part, of a humanitarian character, calculated to increase the income of the submerged sixth so that they might enjoy a standard of living more nearly commensurate with the social ideal of the reformers. Unquestionably, here too the philosophic impulse of the historic movement played a part in the incorporation of this feature in the National Industrial Recovery Act. Equally important, however, was the desire on the part of the administration to use this technique as a means of increasing the purchasing power of the masses. If all other wages could be held the same, and those who worked on the lowest income scale could by common agreement on the part of business have their incomes increased, an increase in the sum total purchasing power of the nation, so it was argued, would result. Just why this should be so may at first glance seem bewildering. Nevertheless, all other things being equal, it can probably be taken for granted that a larger percentage of a wage-earners' income, particularly of those incomes which would be increased by the minimum-wage provision, is spent for consumption purposes than is the case with those incomes which fall in the upper brackets of the income tax.

The question inevitably arose as to where the employer was to obtain the funds necessary to meet these increased payrolls. The answer given by the administration was fourfold in character. In part, from the banks, in part from existing profits, in part from the increase in business activity which a tremendous program of government spending might be expected to bring, and in part from the wage increases themselves. (Of this more anon.)

The stimulation of labor-union organization had likewise a twofold purpose. It was first a step in the direction of industrial democracy. The proponents of the National Industrial Recovery Act believed, that "the establishment of this measure of parliamentary government within industrial life, in which there is representation of all significant interests, has made it possible to put an end to the state of warfare that existed before, in which consumers, employers, and workers were all balanced against one another under the rather ineffectual regulations of largely negative admonitory laws passed by the government. In other words, it has replaced a system by which the government attempted to police industry from without." The second purpose which lay behind the stimulation and encouragement of organized labor was, however, the more important—the building up of support for the major steps already taken, the reduction of the working-week and the establishment of minimum-wage provisions in the codes. Equally significant, perhaps, was the fact that in the development of the labor unions lay the possibility of introducing into the American scene a force which might conceivably be productive of a better balance between the incomes of the consuming and investing classes in the future.

One might point out parenthetically that the elimination of child labor, the reduction of working-hours, and the establishment of a minimum wage were all steps away from the philosophy of *laissez-faire* with its belief in the efficacy and desirability of the unrestricted operation of economic laws. They were steps, incidentally, which by virtue of their imposition of increased costs of production upon American industry placed us, in so far as these factors are concerned, in a disadvantageous position with regard to international competition. They were steps, consequently, in the direction of intra-nationalism. Nor was the development of powerful labor unions bent on the maintenance of the gains which have been made and the attainment of still others in the future a reversal of this trend.

In its attempt to abolish unfair competition among business men and to introduce a modicum of planning into our industrial system, however, the National Industrial Recovery Act has taken the most radical step away from *laissez-faire* which has yet been taken in America. This aspect of the Act is in part an outgrowth of the line of thought which was responsible for the establishment and maintenance of the Federal Trade Commission; in part, it is a logical development from the trade-association movement, and in part the result of the propaganda of our economic planners, Stuart Chase, Gerard Swope, and others who have seriously studied the problem.

These, then, were the primary objectives of the National Industrial Recovery Act: the spreading of work among the adult unemployed through the elimination of child labor and a radical reduction of working-hours; increasing the purchasing power of the masses through the establishment of minimum wages; the stimulation of labor-union organizations; the abolition of unfair competition among business men; and the introduction of at least a modicum of planning into industry.

CHAPTER SEVENTEEN

THE NATIONAL RECOVERY ADMINISTRATION

To EFFECTUATE the policy of this title, the President is hereby authorized to establish such agencies, to accept and utilize such voluntary and uncompensated services, to appoint, without regard to the provisions of the civil service laws, such officers and employes, and to utilize such Federal officers and employes, and with the consent of the State, such State and local officers and employes, as he may find necessary, to prescribe their authorities, duties, responsibilities, and tenure, and without regard to the Classification Act of 1923, as amended, to fix the compensation of any officers and employes so appointed.

The President may delegate any of his functions and powers under this title to such officers, agents, and employes as he may designate or appoint, and may establish an industrial planning and research agency to aid in carrying out his functions under this title.

In these words the National Recovery Administration was forecast.

Heading the National Recovery Administration, as well as all other branches of the national administration, stands the President. Immediately under him in the National Recovery Administration is the National Recovery Administrator, General Hugh Johnson. Two personal advisers, an Assistant Administrator for Industry and an Assistant Administrator for Labor, come next in the hierarchy. Immediately below these personal advisers come the Divisional Administrators, the heads of the five great divisions—the division of extractive industries, textile trades, metals, chemicals, and transportation and amusements. Whether the division of transportation and amusements should be put on a plane of equality with the other four divisions it is difficult to state. It is of more recent origin, and, down to date, at least, has not occupied a position of equal importance.

One should perhaps parenthesize here the remark that it is exceedingly difficult even yet to chart the organization of the National Recovery Administration, first, because the organization is still in a flux, and second, because the lines of authority and responsibility have not been sharply drawn.

Under the Divisional Administrators and, theoretically, at least, responsible to them are the Deputy Administrators in charge of specific codes, the formulation of which is in their hands.

The heart of the National Industrial Recovery Act, it should perhaps be stated parenthetically, lies in the codes of fair practices which have been and are being formulated. Through them child labor has been eliminated, hours of labor regulated, and minimum-wage scales established. Through them an attempt is being made, it is said, to introduce a modicum of planning into industry. Violations of the standards of fair competition thus set up in connection with any transaction affecting interstate commerce are deemed unfair methods of competition subject to the penalties of the law.

Despite the fact that the majority of the codes have long since been formulated, a detailed analysis of the procedure followed in their formulation is, nevertheless, significant. A number of codes, be it said, are still in the process of formulation.

The initial step in the formulation of a code of fair practices has rested, as the procedure has worked out, with each individual industry. Once the industry has whipped its proposed code into shape, it has gone to the Deputy Administrator in charge of the particular industry. Hearings have been held and the points of view of dissident minorities within the industry have been considered. Advice has then been sought and obtained from the Division of Research and Planning, the Legal Division, the Industrial Advisory Board, the Labor Advisory Board, and the Consumers' Advisory Board. In a very loose sense the question of what shall go into a particular code, however, is determined by the Deputy Administrator in charge.

As finally formulated by the deputy, the code should theoretically pass under the scrutiny of the Divisional Administrator, although in point of fact not all codes have done so. Protests against various items included in a particular code may be filed with him, and he in turn may make such changes in the code as he in his discretion deems wise.

The Divisional Administrator now turns the code, as it has thus far been formulated, over to General Johnson, the National Recovery Administrator, who may likewise make such changes as he sees fit. Down until quite recently all codes went directly to the President for final acceptance. A recent presidential order has made General Johnson the court of final arbitration in drafting the remaining codes. His adjudication of all disputes which have not been settled by the Deputy Administrator and the Divisional Administrator, and which are of sufficient importance to be appealed to him, is consequently definitive.

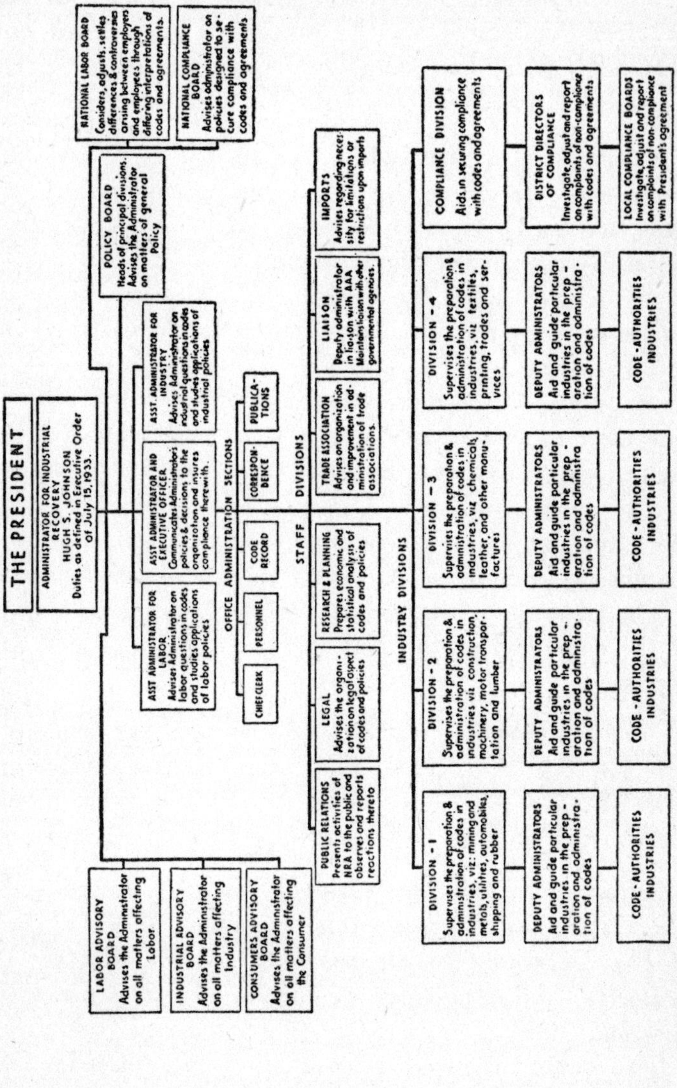
THE PRESIDENT
ADMINISTRATOR FOR INDUSTRIAL RECOVERY HUGH S. JOHNSON Duties as defined in Executive Order of July 15, 1933.
NATIONAL LABOR BOARD Considers, adjusts, settles differences & controversies arising between employers and employees through differing interpretations of codes and agreements.
NATIONAL COMPLIANCE BOARD Advises administrator on policies designed to secure compliance with codes and agreements
POLICY BOARD Heads of principal divisions. Advises the Administrator on matters of general Policy
ASST. ADMINISTRATOR FOR LABOR Advises Administrator on labor questions in codes and studies applications of labor policies
ASST. ADMINISTRATOR AND EXECUTIVE OFFICER Communicates Administrator's policies & decisions to the organization and insures compliance therewith.
ASST. ADMINISTRATOR FOR INDUSTRY Advises Administrator on industrial questions in codes and studies applications of industrial policies
OFFICE ADMINISTRATION SECTIONS
CHIEF CLERK
PERSONNEL
CODE RECORD
CORRESPONDENCE
PUBLICATIONS
STAFF DIVISIONS
PUBLIC RELATIONS Presents activities of NRA to the public and observes and reports reactions thereto
LEGAL Advises the organization on legal aspect of codes and policies
RESEARCH & PLANNING Prepares economic and statistical analysis of codes and policies
TRADE ASSOCIATION Advises on organization and improvement in administration of trade associations.
LIAISON Deputy administrator in liaison with AAA. Maintains liaison with other governmental agencies.
IMPORTS Advises regarding necessity for limitations or restrictions upon imports
INDUSTRY DIVISIONS
DIVISION - 1 Supervises the preparation & administration of codes in industries, viz: mining and metals, utilities, automobiles, shipping and rubber
DIVISION - 2 Supervises the preparation & administration of codes in industries viz construction, machinery, motor transportation and lumber
DIVISION - 3 Supervises the preparation & administration of codes in industries, viz chemicals, leather, and other manufactures
DIVISION - 4 Supervises the preparation & administration of codes in industries, viz textiles, printing, trades and services
COMPLIANCE DIVISION Aids in securing compliance with codes and agreements
DEPUTY ADMINISTRATORS Aid and guide particular industries in the preparation and administration of codes
DISTRICT DIRECTORS OF COMPLIANCE Investigate, adjust and report on complaints of non-compliance with codes and agreements
CODE-AUTHORITIES INDUSTRIES
LOCAL COMPLIANCE BOARDS Investigate, adjust and report on complaints of non-compliance with President's agreement
LABOR ADVISORY BOARD Advises the Administrator on all matters affecting Labor
INDUSTRIAL ADVISORY BOARD Advises the Administrator on all matters affecting Industry
CONSUMERS ADVISORY BOARD Advises the Administrator on all matters affecting the Consumer

To aid what, for want of a better term, might be called the executive division of the National Recovery Administration, which has just been described, a number of advisory divisions have been established. The most widely publicized of these are the National Industrial *Advisory* Board, the Labor *Advisory* Board, and the Consumers' *Advisory* Board. Equally important, perhaps, are the Division of Research and Planning and the Legal Division. We shall attempt a little later to describe in some detail the work of each of these divisions. Suffice it to say for the moment, the Division of Research and Planning supplies the National Administrator and his deputies with certain facts relative to each industry. The most important of these is a statistical analysis of each proposed code showing the extent to which the adoption of such a code would stimulate reemployment, and the extent to which the minimum-wage scale contained therein would increase the weekly payroll of the industry.

The resources of the Legal Division have likewise been at the command of the National Administrator and his deputies.

The function of the Industrial Advisory Board, the Labor Advisory Board, and the Consumers' Advisory Board, briefly stated, is to assist their respective clients in presenting their respective points of view on each and every code to the Deputy Administrators, the Divisional Administrators and the National Recovery Administrator, in the most effective manner possible. Whether each of these advisory boards has been equally effective in protecting the interest of its clients, however, is a moot question.

Two other divisions remain to be considered: The Compliance Division and the Code Authority Division.

Neither of these divisions has played a part in the formulation of the codes of fair practices. Their importance, nevertheless, looms larger and larger as the days go by. The first of these, the Compliance Division, is essentially the Law Enforcement Division. Under it state and local compliance boards have been organized. In so far as possible it attempts to obtain compliance with the provisions of the codes without resort to penal action. Where this does not prove possible, the enforcement of the law may be turned over to the Federal Trade Commission or to the Attorney-General. No less important is the work of the Code Authority Division. The codes which have been formulated and adopted under the tremendous pressure of the emergency are obviously far from perfect. Many problems remain. The solution of these problems and many others which will inevitably arise is the task of this latter division.

CHAPTER EIGHTEEN

THE RÔLE OF THE DEPUTY-ADMINISTRATORS

In a sense the Deputy-Administrators of the National Recovery Administration have been the big men in the formulation of the codes of fair practices. Nevertheless, it would be easy to over-emphasize their importance.

Although to the average newspaper reader the steps in the formulation of a code of fair practice have appeared simple indeed, such has been far from the case. Nor has the rôle played by the Deputy-Administrator been quite as heroic as that portrayed in the papers. A glance behind the scenes while the code of fair competition for the graphic arts industries (the printing industries) was being formulated may indicate some of the difficulties involved in the formulation of a code and may at the same time present a more accurate picture of the rôle of a deputy than any collection of generalizations possibly could.

Anticipating the passage of the National Industrial Recovery Act, the Industrial Control Committee of the United Typothetæ of America (the national trade association of the book and job branch of the printing industry) began to consider ways and means of cooperating with the Federal government. As a result of its activities a National Conference of Printers was held in Washington on July 22-23, 1933. Not only were the representatives of the book and job branch of the printing industry present, but representatives of some thirty or more other printers' associations as well.

A tentative draft of a basic code for the printing industry was formulated. Before presenting this code to the National Recovery Administration, however, the Washington conference decided to submit it to a somewhat more representative conference of the printing industry. Such a conference was called in Chicago. To it came representatives from some 25,000 independent printing establishments. So acute were the conflicts of interest which appeared at this convention, that amendment after amendment had to be made in the first basic code drafted at Washington in July. Compromise upon compromise had to be effected. And despite all efforts at compromise, the representatives of the National Editorial Association (the trade association for the small country newspapers, many of which combine commercial printing with newspaper printing) walked out of the conference and held a rump convention of their own. As a result, there were presented to the National Recovery Administration two basic codes.

In addition, a number of other codes dealing with subsidiary aspects of the graphic arts industries were presented. Indeed, the notice of public hearings to begin September 18, 1933, listed codes which had been presented by national trade associations representing the book-manufacturing industry, the textbook-publishing industry, the city directory industry, the periodical-publishing industry, the play-publishing industry, the advertising newspaper industry, the loose-leaf manufacturing industry, the label manufacturing industry, the lithographing industry, the photo-lithographing industry, the music-printing industry, the ticket and coupon industry, the greeting-card industry, the security-engraving-and-printing industry, the photoengraving industry, electrotyping, stereotyping, and typesetting industries, and the advertising typography industry. Thus, before the code of fair competition for the graphic arts industries had been finally formulated, almost fifty basic and subsidiary codes had been presented.

Between September 5th and the date set for the hearings, the Deputy Administrator in charge of the code for the graphic arts industries brought the representatives of the United Typothetæ of America and the representatives of the National Editorial Association together again and again. No common agreement could be reached. As a result, when the public hearings began, the Deputy Administrator had before him a draft of a basic code proposed by the United Typothetæ of America and another draft proposed by the National Editorial Association.

At the hearings representatives of the divergent industrial groups publicly presented their points of view. Representatives of the labor unions likewise made their appearance. Such information as the division of research and planning had available was also turned over to the Deputy. The views of the Industrial Advisory Board, the Labor Advisory Board, and the Consumers' Advisory Board were likewise presented. Without intending to minimize unduly the importance of these hearings, the point should be emphasized that the hearings were by no means the crucial steps in code formulation. In so far as they were useful, they were useful merely as a technique of furnishing the Deputy Administrator with factual information he might not otherwise have had, and, more important, as a means of furnishing him with an additional opportunity to size up the various factors present in the situation. The hearings were useful also, it might be said parenthetically, in protecting the National Recovery Administration from legal assault, since the courts have long since laid down the rule that an administrative hearing shall be granted all interested parties before an administrative decision, quasi-legislative in character, may be handed down. Such an attitude on the part of the courts is obviously equitable, for only thus can all dissident groups be guaranteed an opportunity of presenting their views.

Much more important than the hearings in the formulation of the code for the graphic arts industries were the conferences which began upon the conclusion of the hearings and continued at intervals until December, 1933. Early in September these conferences had "all the earmarks of a debating society." Indeed, not until the middle of October did they take on "the aspects of a deliberative assembly." The trouble was that nowhere in the graphic arts industries was there anyone who could speak for the industry as a whole. There were, instead, only spokesmen for special interests within the industry, more interested in protecting their respective constituencies than in advancing the interests of the entire industry—or, one might add, the common weal.

To expedite the business of the conference when it finally did get down to work, its membership was divided into three subdivisions, on wages and working conditions, price stabilization, and administration, respectively. Each subcommittee was so constituted as to be representative of the entire conference. "At intervals," says the conference report, "the chairmen of these subcommittees reported to the meetings of the general conference as to matters of both agreement and disagreement. These reports were then considered by the general assembly, and those parts which were approved were turned over to a code-drafting committee to be incorporated in the basic code. During these weeks several editions of the basic code were considered and discarded. The draft dated October 21, 1933, was submitted to the representatives of labor and long discussions took place over the hours and wage provisions.

"The request of the labor representatives was for higher minimum rates and lower hours. When these discussions proved fruitless, the Administrator spent five days with members of the various graphic arts and labor representatives, and the committees then proceeded to revise the code. A new draft of eighty closely printed pages dated December 7 was considered by the conference which met in Washington on that date and was indorsed so far as fundamentals were concerned, then was considerably revised in many of its details."

To what extent did the Deputy Administrators dominate the scene in these industrial conferences? In one sense, not at all! For, despite the provision in the National Industrial Recovery Act granting the President authority to impose a code upon an industry, no such action was ever taken, nor, for that matter, seriously contemplated. The task of the deputy administrator was essentially that of a negotiator charged with the duty of representing the public interest. He might persuade and cajole the representatives of industry into including provisions within a given code which would not otherwise have appeared. He might refuse to recommend a code unless this item was included, that item stricken out. Without question Deputy Administrators again and again eliminated particularly obnoxious items from the codes in this manner. The number of issues in any one code upon which action of this character could be taken, however, was exceedingly small. By and large, consequently, the rôle of the Deputy Administrator has been that of a negotiator. He has always been faced with the possibility that if he got too far ahead of opinion within an industry, the industry might walk out on him.

In the final analysis, in the formulation of these codes of fair competition the industries have held the whip hand. And, although in a measure the excellence or lack of excellence of a particular code may be related to the abilities or indifference of the deputy who has negotiated it, to a much larger degree the terms of a particular code have been determined by the desires of the majority of an industry, the character of the minority dissent, the nature of the proposing trade associations, and the leadership under which they came to Washington.

CHAPTER NINETEEN

PROTECTING THE CONSUMER

No LESS important than the work of the Deputy Administrator in the formulation of the codes of fair practices has been the work of thc three Advisory Boards, which were designed to present the point of view of the three major interests which constitute our economy. In a sense they were conceived to be a first step in the direction of a partnership between capital, labor, and the consumer.

Of the three the Labor Advisory Board and the Consumers' Advisory Board are the most important. I say this not because they have been the most effective but, because it is self-evident that industry was and is equipped to present its point of view with or without the assistance of the Industrial Advisory Board. As a matter of fact the weak sister of the three has been the Consumers' Advisory Board.

This has been true for a number of reasons. The fact simply is that although the Consumers' Advisory Board was charged by the Administrator of the National Recovery Administration with protecting the interest of the consumer by "watching every agreement and every hearing to see that nothing is done to impair the interest of those whose daily living may be affected by these agreements," the concept of what constitutes the consumer's interest has never been defined. The dismal science of economics has devoted itself to problems of production rather than to those of consumption. Thus, although from the start industry had a definite idea of what it wanted, although labor was cognizant of its major objectives, the consumer had nowhere formulated a realistic program. The Consumers' Advisory Board members were therefore immediately confronted with the task of thinking through a problem of staggering magnitude—unaided by earlier research.

Was it their task to look after the consumers' interests merely in the retail market? Or was it their duty to make a complete check upon industrial processes from the raw material to the finished goods and their distribution to the ultimate consumer? Were they to be exclusively interested in prices? Or did the tremendous question of standards of quality fall within their purview? What position should consumers' representatives take upon certain proposed limitations upon competition, upon open price schedules, upon destructive price-cutting, upon so-called unfair trade practices, upon sales contracts? These were some of the questions which had to be answered before the Advisory Board could hope to function effectively. There was no time for research. The decisions had to be made immediately. It is no wonder, consequently, that the concept of "the consumer's interest" which has been formulated is even yet still far from satisfactory, even to the members of the Board.

Equally important in explaining the seeming ineffectiveness of the Board in its struggle in behalf of the forgotten man, the consumer, is the fact that politically the consumers are unorganized. The organized consumer hardly exists. Had the Consumers' Advisory Board been laboring under no other difficulty, this situation alone would be sufficient to explain a large measure of the

Board's seeming ineffectiveness. It had no organized political support.

Closely allied to this lack of organization was a third difficulty which hampered the work of the Advisory Board. This was primarily administrative in character. Unlike the Industrial Advisory Board and the Labor Advisory Board, the Consumers' Advisory Board had no reservoir of representatives upon which to draw in the presentation of its case to the National Administrator and his deputies. The Industrial Advisory Board had, perhaps, the greatest advantage in this respect. It was able to call upon the captains of industry to assist it in presenting its case. And without question their technical information has been of great assistance to this Board. Nor have the "big names" assembled by the Industrial Advisory Board been without their psychological effect. Similarly, the Labor Advisory Board was able to draw upon the federated labor unions for assistance. The staff of the Consumers' Advisory Board, on the other hand, has had to fight its battle unaided.

A fourth and final difficulty which confronted the Consumers' Advisory Board was largely psychological. The majority of the Deputy Administrators, naturally enough, were drawn from the ranks of industry. In so far as government service was concerned, they were birds of passage. At the end of a few months or a year, most of them returned to the service of industry. For them to dissociate themselves entirely from the industrialists' point of view, consequently, was humanly impossible. Their ability to do so, of course, varied from deputy to deputy. The fact remains, nevertheless, that, in some degree at least, the cards were stacked against the Consumers' Advisory Board. Despite these handicaps, however, the Consumers'

Advisory Board did some effective work and laid the groundwork for even more effective work in the future. A procedure for the development of quality standards and the accurate labeling of all products has been evolved and urged upon the National Administrator and his deputies.

Although the attitude of the Advisory Board upon the question of price-fixing varied from industry to industry the Board seemingly inclined to the point of view that such a practice should be resorted to only under exceptional circumstances. A memorandum prepared for the use of staff advisers on codes expressed the attitude of the Board quite concisely:

> In dealing with the issue of prices, it is recognized that there is a widespread tendency to try out variants in price determination falling between competition as unfolded in the past, and something approaching public-utility regulation. The Board's advisers should be open-minded in dealing with such proposals, and, in gauging them, should give great weight to their potentialities in generating greater consumption and output during the emergency. But they should be mindful that the history of price-fixing by private enterprise is a dismal one, viewed either from the public point of view or from that of enterprises jointly engaged in it. They should also bear in mind that price-fixing by public authority, such as that in the field of utilities, involves techniques which thus far have not been applied very successfully to the protection of the consumer. The record of price-fixing is such, however, that *whenever it is proposed to increase private power to control prices it should be vigorously urged that this grant be accompanied by arrangements for public control competent to cope with this greater power.*

The Advisory Board has likewise gone on record as opposing the allocation of production among existing industrial plants except under unusual conditions. It has also urged that "representatives of the public, and not of the industry, determine the quantities to be produced and their allocation; that, in making allocation, emphasis be placed upon such factors as amounts of product needed by other industries and the relative efficiency of producing units rather than existing investments and plant capacities; and that the system of allocation be clearly recognized as a temporary expedient and be coupled with a plan for the permanent reorganization of the industry." The Board, similarly, has opposed the writing into the codes of any restrictions on new plants and machinery and has urged that such action be made "the subject of a considered and consistent declaration of national policy."

Although the Board is by no means satisfied that it has entirely thought through its position, it is evident that considerable strides have been made.

The task of presenting the point of view of the Advisory Board to the National Administrator and his deputies has fallen for the most part upon the permanent staff of the Board, although some assistance was obtained from certain purchasing agents attached to large retail houses. The staff was for this purpose broken up into five sections; an executive division; one devoted to an analysis of the codes; another, to complaints; a third, to price investigations; and still another to economic education. The executive division directs the operation of the entire staff and constitutes the clearing point between the Consumers' Advisory Board and other sections of the National Recovery Administration as well as the general public.

The section on economic education was designed to aid in the organization of consumers' councils in the three thousand counties throughout the United States.

The price-investigation section has made studies of prices under the codes for the specific use of consumers' advisers and has assembled such information as was necessary for the handling of complaints.

The complaints section has answered consumer complaints and compiled and tabulated information for the use of the code advisers.

The code section, however, has been the division which has been on the firing-line. The members of this section have analyzed the codes from the consumers' angle. They have attended the preliminary hearings on the codes before the Deputy Administrators and have presented the consumers' point of view. They have attended the public hearings on each and every code and have read into the record their analyses of each code. They have participated to a degree in the post-hearing conferences. Finally, they have presented their recommendations to the Consumers' Advisory Board to be filed with the Divisional Administrator and the National Administrator.

Frequently—one might say, usually—they have been over-ruled. Their recommendations have been rejected. Nevertheless three things are evident: first, save for the watchfulness of the representatives of the Consumers' Advisory Board, the position of the consumer would have received even less consideration than it did in the formulation of these codes of fair competition; second, the groundwork has been laid for the second period of code formulation which is now in progress, a period of code revision. Written into the record are facts and arguments which are certainly receiving more consideration at the present moment than they did when they were presented, facts which may be expected to receive even more consideration in the future, when the effects of the errors of the present have made themselves even more clearly felt. Finally, there has been established an administrative agency, dedicated to the interest of the consumers, which may be expected to play a larger and larger rôle in days to come.

CHAPTER TWENTY

FIGHTING FOR LABOR

MUCH more effective than the work of the Consumers' Advisory Board has been that of the Labor Advisory Board. Its greater effectiveness may be explained in part by the fact that its objectives have been somewhat more clearly defined, and in part by the fact that it has had the powerful political backing of organized labor.

The objectives of the Labor Advisory Board may be summarized briefly: (1) the elimination of child labor; (2) shorter hours; (3) higher wages; (4) improved working conditions; (5) the protection of the right of labor to collective bargaining; (6) the appointment of a representative of labor to each of the code or enforcement authorities; (7) the establishment within each industry of a committee on labeling and standards; and (8) the grant of sufficient power to each code authority to enable it to obtain from the members of the industry such information as may be required for code administration and enforcement.

Simple and well defined though these objectives appear, their attainment has been in fact a matter of the utmost complexity. The mere question of hours and wages may, perhaps, serve as an illustration of the difficulties with which the Board was faced. No attempt has been made to introduce absolute uniformity into the codes with regard to maximum hours or minimum wages, either within a given industry or between industries. The question inevitably arises, why not?

Any attempt to do so would have done one of two things: it would either have caused such a terrific readjustment of our industrial life as to throw business after business into bankruptcy, or it would have been totally ineffective in accomplishing its main objective—the reabsorption of the unemployed into industry.

What would have been the fate of the laundry industry throughout the South, for example, if a uniform six-hour day and five-day week, together with a uniform minimum wage of twelve or fourteen dollars per week, had been adopted? At the time when the laundry code was formulated many Southern laundries were paying their help four or five dollars a week for an eight- or nine-hour day. The question involved, remember, is not the equity of the existing situation. It is, what would have been the consequence of introducing a six-hour day and a five-day week, coupled with a minimum wage of from twelve to fourteen dollars a week? The cost of operating these laundries would have tripled. One of two results would inevitably have followed: either a falling off in the demand for laundry service and the bankruptcy of laundry after laundry —with the consequent discharge of employes—or the mechanization of the laundry processes with an equally inevitable discharge of employes.

But why introduce a six-hour day and a five-day week? Why not a seven-hour day and six-day week? Or an eight-hour day, and a five-day week? Under these latter provisions, industries which could stand a reduction of working hours to thirty or thirty-five a week without undue disturbance to their position in the community would have been totally unaffected. Thousands of men who might otherwise readily have been reabsorbed by them would have continued to find themselves in the ranks of the unemployed.

For a time, at least, it seemed wisest for the Labor Advisory Board to insist, not on a uniform reduction of working-hours and a uniform minimum wage, but rather upon such a reduction in working-hours and such a minimum wage as each industry could stand.

The task of the code analyst of the Labor Advisory Board, consequently, was to calculate the adequacy of the maximum hours in each proposed code in the light of (a) the number of jobless in the industry, (b) the peak periods of employment, (c) the existence of overtime, (d) the hours in other industries, and (e) the character of the occupation.

Although the calculation of hours of labor and minimum-wage rates was perhaps the most complicated burden placed upon the Labor Advisory Board and its staff, a thousand and one other questions remained. Should a differentiation in hours be made for the clerical force, night watchmen, outside salesmen, emergency and repair crews, women, or handicapped workers? What attitude should be taken toward piecework, toward wage differentials by localities, toward weekly, bi-weekly or monthly payments, toward vacations? What specific provisions in the codes would best eliminate the most flagrant abuses of labor in each industry—labor camps unfit for human occupation, excessive transportation charges, charges to workers for tools and supplies, excessive deductions for meals, company stores, etc.? What safeguards could be established to prevent the widespread use of learners and beginners as a means of breaking down the minimum-wage provisions?

Although some fifty-two persons constituted the staff of the Labor Advisory Board, approximately half of whom belonged to the professional class, the executive director and the four chief code analysts assumed the major responsibility.

The preliminary hearings on each code have been attended by one of the code analysts, or by a representative of labor drawn from one of the labor unions, or by both. At the end of the preliminary hearing, both the labor representative and the code analyst have written reports on the proposed code. The report of the labor representative has usually been incorporated by the analyst in the final draft of his report to the Labor Advisory Board. On the basis of these reports, a statement drawn up by the staff of the Labor Advisory Board has been read at the public hearings.

More important than the formal hearings, however, have been the post-hearing conferences. These have been the meetings at which all differences in points of view have been ironed out. And here, of necessity, a great deal of bargaining has taken place. The task of the representative of labor, bluntly put, has been to get all he can for labor.

When the code has been finally drafted, the code analyst in charge has made a detailed analysis of the code, provision by provision. This analysis has been sent to the deputy to use as he sees fit. The code has then been returned to the Labor Advisory Board once again, where it has been gone over by the senior adviser, the executive director, and the chairman of the Board. If the code violated in any fundamental way the principles adopted by the Labor Advisory Board as the minimum it would accept, or if changes were desired, a further communication was sent to the Deputy Administrator in charge of the code, and to the Divisional Administrator in charge.

The Deputy Administrator and possibly the Divisional Chief would then get in touch with the chairman of the Labor Advisory Board, or with its executive director, and defend the code as it stood or agree to the changes requested. If no agreement could be reached, or if a deputy was simply unreasonable, a meeting of the entire Labor Advisory Board was called and the situation placed before it. Such action was thought to carry more weight than action by the chairman of the Board alone.

The failure of a deputy to secure the approval of the Labor Advisory Board for the labor provisions of any code he might have in charge meant that he would have the task of justifying these provisions both to the National Recovery Administrator and to the President. The Labor Advisory Board has, in fact, been successful in presenting and winning its case nine times out of ten. The codes of fair competition contain, for the most part, as satisfactory labor provisions as the Labor Advisory Board has believed it possible to work out. Despite this seeming success, however, a number of interesting questions remain.

Did the Labor Advisory Board achieve its extraordinary success because it set itself an exceedingly conservative goal? Was this politically expedient or would the very opposite course have been wiser?

Why did the Labor Advisory Board not give greater support to the Consumers' Advisory Board? Of what utility is it to increase wages if an unjustifiable increase in the cost of living offsets any mometary gains which have been made?

Why did the Labor Advisory Board not fight more vigorously than it did for a representative of both labor and the consumer on each of the code authorities?

Why was a wage differential permitted between North and South? If this differential was based on a differential in living costs why could not a better measure have been found?

These questions are not raised for the purpose of detracting from the praise which may justly be accorded the Labor Advisory Board for a task well done, but merely to indicate that the battle for labor has by no means been completely won.

CHAPTER TWENTY-ONE

PROTECTING INDUSTRY

In view of the adequacy with which industry can present its own point of view, the function of the Industrial Advisory Board is at first glance a mystery. Nor does the Presidential mandate that the Advisory Board shall "be responsible in that every affected industrial group be fully and adequately represented in an advisory capacity" entirely clarify the situation. The Board itself early interpreted its mandate to mean that there had been imposed upon it the duty of informing industry of its rights, privileges, and responsibilities in code preparation and administration.

In the case of some industries this has meant the holding of preliminary conferences for the purpose of ironing out some of the problems of trade organization and representation. In others it has meant the exposition to the members of an industry of the privileges and duties of industry under the National Recovery Act. "Even now," as a member of the staff of the Industrial Advisory Board put it, "some trades present codes which do not take full advantage of the opportunity to make an advance in industrial self-government. They apparently do not see possibilities offered by NRA in making new and greater steps forward in united attacks on trade evils." It means, in other words, the protection of industry against itself.

The industrial adviser checks over the labor provisions,

the trade practices, the administrative articles, and other sections of each code to see that the industry has not "tied itself up in knots." Specifically, if, in the formulation of its code, a particular industry has not included provisions allowing for a wage rate lower than the minimum for handicapped persons or hours greater than the maximum for watchmen, the industrial adviser suggests their inclusion.

Equally important has been the Board's function as the adviser to the administrator on general problems of industrial organization, trends, methods, and viewpoints. Its task has been to present a broad business attitude as distinct from that of any particular group. What was the limit of cooperation that industry could offer under the President's reemployment agreement or blanket code? What is the proper relationship between the trade association in industry and the code authority and the government? How should the government representatives on the code authority be appointed? Is there economic need for the control of production or limitation on plant capacity? Are geographical wage differentials desirable? Will the competitive positions of small firms be jeopardized under National Recovery Administration operations? Is government financing of small firms necessary during the period of adjustment to National Recovery Administration?

These and a hundred other questions have arisen. Together with the Consumers' Advisory Board and the Labor Advisory Board, the Industrial Advisory Board has presented its answer. And, as might have been anticipated by virtue of the mandate laid upon it to present the industrial point of view, its recommendations have not always coincided with the viewpoint of its sister boards.

These, briefly, have been the characteristics of the Industrial Advisory Board which have differentiated it from an attorney for industry.

The Industrial Advisory Board differs in composition from its two sister advisory boards in that, until very recently, one-third of its members retired every four months. Thus, in fact there has been a new advisory board every year. The purpose of this arrangement has been threefold: first, the introduction of new blood into government service; second, the education of the leaders of industry in the aims and purposes of the National Recovery Administration; and, third, the distribution of the burden of this advisory service among a large number of people. Unlike some of the other advisory boards, the Industrial Advisory Board has itself passed on each and every provision in each and every code. Consequently, it has been in more or less continuous session. To request such intensive voluntary service from anyone for more than four months would, obviously, have been an imposition.

In similar fashion, the staff of the Industrial Advisory Board has differed from the staffs of the other two advisory boards in that it has been made up of presidents and vice-presidents of large and small corporations. These men have likewise been on a volunteer basis. Their stay in the government service has usually been for a period of months only—sufficiently long, however, for them to familiarize themselves with the proceedings of the National Recovery Administration and to handle such codes as might be assigned to them, from their initial formulation to their final acceptance by the President.

The question might be asked as to whether these men represent an industrial or a social point of view. One is assured on all sides that they are distinctly socially-minded. Nevertheless, as one questions further, the fact is quickly revealed that for the most part they have had what might be called a reasonably enlightened business man's view, rather than the point of view of the consumer or the point of view of labor. This, perhaps, in itself raises the question, "What is a social point of view?" Limits of space fortunately prevent any attempt to answer the question here.

The procedure followed by the Industrial Advisory Board in presenting its point of view to the Deputy Administrators, to the Divisional Administrators and to the National Recovery Administrator has differed very little from the procedure followed by the boards we have previously discussed. One of the "resident advisers" has attended the preliminary hearings and has participated in such discussion as arose. Similarly, he has attended the public hearings and has presented such facts as seemed pertinent. Likewise, he has participated in the post-hearing conferences and has aided and assisted the representatives of the industry concerned in every way possible. Finally, he has made an analysis of the code as far as it has been formulated, and has presented his report to the Industrial Advisory Board.

After going over his report the Board has made such recommendations to the Deputy Administrator and to the divisional chief as seemed to them desirable. Representatives of the Advisory Board, likewise, have participated in such later discussions relative to fair trade practices and to such other items in the proposed code as have arisen, urging the point of view of the Advisory Board upon the Deputy Administrator, the Divisional Administrator, and the National Recovery Administrator, until such time as an agreement has finally been reached and a decision finally made.

To what extent the accident of "big names" among the code analysts of the Industrial Advisory Board has had a psychological effect upon the Deputy Administrators and the Divisional Administrators in their decisions as to what they should recommend to the National Administrator and to the President, it is difficult to determine.

How successful the work of the Industrial Advisory Board has been likewise is difficult of measurement. One may nevertheless hazard the guess that from the point of view of the industrialist, it has been exceedingly satisfactory.

Whether, from a long-range point of view, the Industrial Advisory Board might not have displayed a higher statesmanship if it had thrown its influence behind the Consumers' Advisory Board in the latter's demand for more effective safeguards for the consumer, time alone can tell.

CHAPTER TWENTY-TWO

INDUSTRY'S INNER CONFLICT

WHETHER or not the Marxians are right that the great cleavage of society in the future—over-shadowing all else—will be the division between capital and labor, such is certainly not the case in America today. And nowhere has that fact been more strikingly revealed than in connection with the formulation of the codes of fair competition. There is, of course, a conflict between labor and capital. Similarly, there is a fundamental divergence of interest between the producer and the consumer. Nevertheless, cutting across these broad interests are a thousand and one subordinate but, in a sense, more intense loyalties around which large segments of our industrial society have rallied. A *mêlée*, not a battle, has been and is in progress. So complicated is the scene, in fact, so varied is the strife that one cannot help wondering whether General Johnson and his Deputy Administrators have not long since yearned for that Elysian society in which the only battle would be the conflict between capital and labor. To act as an umpire in such a society would be a simple thing indeed in comparison with the difficulty of acting as an arbiter of the conflicting interests in the American industrial order of the present day. One need but list the four hundred codes which have already been formulated, without making any reference to the hundred or so more still to come, to indicate something of the complexity of modern society. It seems very improbable that the mop-stick industry, for instance, will ever assume a place of importance within the great society commensurate with that of steel or coal. Nevertheless, a sufficient divergence of interest exists between the mop-stick industry and the other branches of industry to warrant the formulation of a separate code.

How real is the divergence of interest within industry is graphically illustrated by the bitter fight which has been going on between the retailers and the manufacturers. Conceiving their economic interests to be closely allied with those of the consumer, the retailers have been fighting tooth and nail each and every effort of the manufacturers to raise prices through the introduction of certain aspects of monopoly control into the industrial picture. Indeed, it is hardly going too far to say that the chief aid and assistance the Consumers' Advisory Board has thus far received has come from the retailers. Self-interest and not philanthropy, however, has motivated these retail organizations. They have felt, and quite correctly in all probability, that the retailers will handle a larger or smaller volume of business in inverse ratio to prices. They fear the development of manufacturing monopolies so powerful as to be able to control the retailer's margin of profit and reduce him to the rank of a mere agent. There is here, in other words, a real divergence of interest.

This is not the end of the story. Just as formidable are the conflicts which have developed between whole industries. For some time past the rayon industry has been making heavy inroads into the market previously held by the cotton trade. True, it has previously cost more to produce rayon goods than it has to produce cotton. Rayon has, nevertheless, been quite successful in its competition with cotton on the basis of style alone. Both the rayon and the cotton codes have recently been adopted, with the result that the cost of manufacturing certain cotton goods which formerly held the field against rayon has now risen to the place where producers of rayon can actually undersell the cotton textile manufacturers, simply on the basis of manufacturing costs. It is no wonder, consequently, that a certain section of the cotton textile trade insists that the two codes must be readjusted on a basis more equitable to the cotton manufacturer.

On an earlier page the question is raised as to why the Labor Advisory Board had not given greater support to the Consumers' Advisory Board in its battle in behalf of the consumer. On the surface at least it seems rather futile for the Labor Advisory Board to battle for increased wages merely to have the increases offset by an unjustifiable increase in the cost of living. The explanation of this attitude on the part of the Labor Advisory Board turns on one point. There is no such thing in the United States as a consciousness of solidarity either on the part of labor or on the part of the consumer.

A situation which existed in the coal fields some time ago may serve to illustrate this point. The operators in one of the coal fields were reported to have cut prices in an endeavor to expand their output. It was probable, consequently, that the operators in the other fields would be forced to follow suit; thus a downward movement of bituminous coal prices might well have started. If this had taken place, it would only have been a question of time before one operator or another would have slashed wages, and competitive wage slashing would inevitably have followed. The prevention of price-cutting between fields in the bituminous-coal industry thus appeared as imperative to the coal-miners as it did to the operators. Had the technique of price-fixing been the only method of ending this price war, the Labor Advisory Board would undoubtedly have given its assent if not its enthusiastic approval.

But, one may ask, do not the miners realize that in indorsing a policy of price-fixing they are decreasing their own real wages, for they are, after all, consumers as well as producers? True! But the increase in the cost of living which a coal-miner will have to endure by virtue of a policy of price-fixing in the bituminous-coal industry will amount at the most to 1 per cent. This will be true even if, through a policy of price-fixing, the price of coal should be maintained a full 10 per cent above the level to which the force of competition might otherwise drive it, since it is very dubious whether any miner spends as much as 10 per cent of his total income upon coal.

Faced, then, with the alternative of accepting a reduction in his real wages of 1 per cent or less by virtue of a policy of price-fixing or accepting a wage cut of 10, 15, or 20 per cent, the miners certainly will favor price-fixing. They are consumers, but they are producers, too. Nor will the fact that their action will decrease the standard of living of labor generally cause the slightest deviation in their reasoning.

A consciousness of the solidarity of interest upon the part of either labor or the consumer simply does not exist in the United States.

The activities of the National Recovery Administration have clearly revealed that at the moment, at least, we are not divided into the two broad classes—capital and labor, but instead we are organized into tens of thousands, if not hundreds of thousands, of economic groups, each with interests separate and distinct from the interests of other groups. Any changes which are likely to affect the relative economic position of the group to which we belong we look upon with approval or disapproval, according to whether or not such action will advance the interests of our particular group rather than the interests of our particular class. Under certain conditions we federate with other groups for the purpose of advancing any interest we may have in common, but our group alliances are loosely knit, our industrial loyalties, perhaps even our class allegiances, lightly held. As in the case of the coal-miners, we may today be fighting on the side of labor, tomorrow we may be fighting on the side of capital. Like the retailer, we may today be fighting on the side of the producer, tomorrow on the side of the consumer.

Whether it will be possible to adjudicate fairly the conflicting aspirations of these thousands upon thousands of divergent groups remains to be seen. Whether, under a democratic form of government, it will be possible to enforce the decisions once they have been rendered, the future alone will reveal.

CHAPTER TWENTY-THREE

THE DILEMMA OF SMALL BUSINESS

OUT of the work of the National Recovery Administration, out of the *mêlée* of conflicting interests, have evolved some four or five hundred codes. Under their provisions, child labor has been eliminated, hours of labor have been shortened, minimum wage scales have been established and unfair trade practices have been prohibited. By virtue of their formulation, however, certain new problems have arisen, not least among which is the status of the small business man in our economy.

In so far as the small business man has hitherto survived under the competitive system through a ruthless exploitation of child and adult labor, his days are numbered. And few there are who will mourn his passing. If the only claim to managerial ability a small business man can advance is a superior capacity in browbeating labor, the sooner he is eliminated from the managerial class the better. It seems reasonably certain, however, that the burden of the codes rests more heavily on the smaller business man than it does on his larger competitors.

In the first place, the cost of labor is frequently greater in a small establishment than it is in a larger one. This is true for the reason that the medium-sized *entrepreneur* often cannot afford to put in the expensive labor-saving machinery which is to be found in the factories of his great competitors. Thus, the increase in labor costs which has been brought about by the codes is proportionately larger for the little fellow than it is for the great industrialist.

In the second place, the degree of flexibility which can be introduced into a business organization is in some industries in inverse ratio to its personnel. If the shortening of hours of labor under the code of a particular industry means a 20-per-cent curtailment of working-hours for the individual employe this may mean only a slightly increased personnel and a shuffling of the hours of the existing personnel in a large establishment. This will frequently not be the case in a smaller enterprise. An organization employing only eight men, faced with the necessity of rendering the same service, despite a 20-per-cent reduction in hours of labor, may very easily find it necessary to employ two additional men. A reshuffling of hours of the character possible in a great industrial enterprise may be totally impossible in such a case.

Third, the partial suspension of the anti-trust laws may, as the codes now stand, lead to the further development of industrial combinations in certain specific industries. This development may or may not lead to greater efficiency. In so far as it does, the small business man, already handicapped by a relatively greater burden imposed on him by the codes, will have to face an even more intense competition than ever before.

Mention might also be made of the danger to the small business man latent in certain of the variations of price-fixing which have been introduced into the codes, should the code authorities be dominated by the great industrialists. Prices may easily be fixed in such a way as to wipe out a large proportion of the smaller establishments in a given industry. The fact that provisions have been introduced into certain of the codes prohibiting the introduction of additional or improved machinery may actually prevent the smaller *entrepreneur* from increasing his efficiency at the very time that increased labor costs make it imperative for him to do so.

The question arises, moreover, as to where the money is to come from with which the employer is to meet the added labor costs. The answer the Administration has given is, first, from the profits of the business; second, from the corporate surpluses; third, from the banks; and fourth, from government spending. Unfortunately for many a small business man, the effect of government spending has still to be felt. There are no small profits. And in the case of many a small business enterprise, there is no corporate surplus. Moreover, in many parts of the country the banks simply will not advance the necessary credits to the small industrialist or to the small retailer.

Whether this attitude on the part of the banks is due to the fact that the welfare of their own financial structures is inextricably interwoven with the welfare of big business, which, in many industries, would be happy to see the independent *entrepreneur* go to the wall, or whether it is because our commercial banks are simply dubious as to the financial wisdom of lending their depositors' money to the small businesses which make demands upon them, is a moot question. The fact is that in many parts of the country the banks will not extend to the small and medium-sized business man the credits which are imperative if he is to carry on under the rules laid down by the National Recovery Administration.

These, then, are some of the apparent consequences of the codification of industry.

Nor are they entirely hypothetical. The President's Reemployment Agreement specifically exempted from the provisions of the blanket code all businesses, located in towns less than 2,500 and not employing more than two persons. A further modification of that code, made on October 23, 1933, provided as follows:

> The provisions of the President's Reemployment Agreement, issued July 27, 1933, shall not be held to apply to employers engaged only locally in retail trade or in local service industries (and not in a business in or affecting interstate commerce) who do not employ more than five persons and who are located in towns of less than 2,500 population (according to the 1930 Federal census) which are not in the immediate trade area of a city of larger population, except so far as such employers who have signed the President's Reemployment Agreement desire to continue to comply with the terms of said agreement after the date of this order; . . .

More recently all attempts to codify the service industries have been abandoned, and still further exemptions have been extended to employers in small towns.

At the last session of Congress, moreover, the Reconstruction Finance Corporation and the Federal Reserve Banks were authorized to extend loans directly to industry.

In this fashion the Administration indicated its realization of the predicament of many small business men and attempted to alleviate their situation. Whether these innovations will prove adequate to the exigencies of the situation, or whether further action will be necessary, the future alone will reveal.

Although thus conceding that a somewhat inequitable burden has been imposed upon the smaller business man, proponents of the Administration insist that, far from being crushed by the National Recovery Administration, he is in fact better off than before. Along with the bigger business man, the smaller *entrepreneur* has reaped whatever benefits the National Industrial Recovery Act and the allied recovery measures have conferred. The downward rush of the depression has been stopped. There has been some pick-up in business. Thousands of small as well as large business men who might have been driven to the wall have been saved.

And, if the reasoning of the Administration is correct, if increased purchasing power means increased business activity, it is probable, as the protagonists of the Administration insist, that sooner or later the existing financial pressure upon little business and big business alike will abate. Both may once again enjoy a measure of prosperity unknown to the United States since 1929. Whether or not this prosperity lies "just around the corner" depends, of course, upon the validity of the purchasing-power theory upon which considerable portions of the Roosevelt program are predicated.

CHAPTER TWENTY-FOUR

PURCHASING POWER

THE validity of the purchasing-power theory on which the National Recovery Act—and for that matter a considerable portion of the recovery program—is in large measure predicated, is by no means conceded by all economic experts.

Briefly stated, the reasoning of the proponents of the purchasing-power theory is as follows: The wheels of industry can be kept turning only so long as there is a demand for industrial products. It is imperative, consequently, that a sufficient proportion of the national income go to the consuming classes so that the potential output of our productive machinery may be absorbed. In the event that such a policy is not followed, in the event that an undue proportion of the national income falls into the hands of the investing rather than of the consuming class, this money finds its way sooner or later into the development of new mines and the construction of new factories. Although the immediate consequence of this may be the stimulation of employment in the heavy industries and in the building trades, the final outcome is catastrophic, for once the new construction has been completed and the new factories put into operation, they merely add their output to an output already greater than the demand.

Prices fall, profits fall, wages are cut, plants close,

purchasing power is still further contracted, and a depression has started. In the normal course of events, business after business goes through bankruptcy, writing off capital costs and cutting prices until such time as an equilibrium between purchasing power and output has once again been established, that is, until the price level has so far fallen below the income level of the consuming classes that they can once again absorb the output of industry. The problem in normal times is, therefore, to prevent such a maladjustment in the distribution of income between the consuming and investing classes from arising.

In an economic order in which the productive capacity is already greater than the demand, the problem is one of diverting to those two classes that proportion of the national income sufficient to reestablish and maintain a perfect equilibrium.

The question inevitably arises as to who constitute these two classes of society. Are we not all consumers? True! And an exact line of demarcation is difficult to draw. A distinction, nevertheless, can be made. An adult factory hand endeavoring to support a wife and children on ten or twelve dollars a week can obviously save little or nothing. His entire income must of necessity be spent on consumption goods. It seems reasonable, therefore, to place him in the consuming classes. Such is not the case, needless to say, of those possessed of incomes of one million or more a year. Try as they might it would be impossible for them to spend their incomes on consumption goods. They almost inevitably fall into the investing class. So much is simple. Just where the line should be drawn between these two extremes is, as I have already suggested, difficult to indicate. Nevertheless, it is probably safe to assert that the laboring and lower middle classes spend more and save less of their annual incomes than do the other classes in the community. This, at least, is the line of demarcation the proponents of the purchasing-power theory usually have in mind.

One of the ways of increasing purchasing power, as the proponents of this theory saw it in the days when the recovery program was being formulated, is for industry itself to divert a larger and larger proportion of its income into the hands of the working-classes, and less and less into the hands of the investors. Upon this premise the National Industrial Recovery Act was, in part at least, predicated.

The critics of the purchasing-power theory insist that it tremendously over-simplifies the picture. The fabulous boom of 1928-29 of which the present depression is the unhappy aftermath, they assert, grew out of a maladjustment in our credit structure rather than out of a maladjustment between the consumers' and investors' incomes. In support of their contention they point to the tremendous bank loans against security collateral and the stupendous investments by banks in industrial bonds. They insist that the building boom of 1928-29 was financed not out of savings, but out of credit. They conclude, consequently, that no matter how equally income might have been divided, the result would have been the same.

Nor do the critics of the purchasing-power theory stop here. Figures are marshaled to indicate that far from consuming less than usual in 1929, the American people were actually consuming more. In 1919 the total value of goods and services consumed is said to have been $60,900,000,000; in 1929, $85,300,000,000. In the light of these figures, the critics ask: How is it possible to lay the depression at the door of any theory of under-consumption. Under this attack, the proponents of the under-consumption theory are for the most part inclined to retreat, to admit that purchasing power is but one aspect, albeit they insist the most important aspect, of the situation. They willingly concede that the attainment of just that equilibrium which is desirable between consumption and investment is much more complicated than the mere division of the nation's annual income, and they maintain that the proper control of credit is imperative.

A second assault upon the purchasing-power theory comes from those who see in the Puritanical virtue of saving the desideratum of all economic good. Only through the accumulation of capital, they insist, is it possible to develop the potential resources of the country. The automobile, electricity, the radio, the airplane, and all the other industrial achievements of the age were rendered possible through the existence of sufficient capital to develop and perfect them. To slow up the accumulation of capital, then, is to slow up the development of new industries and the perfection of old ones.

Two consequences will inevitably follow: first, many of those normally engaged in the heavy industries will, of necessity, find themselves permanently unemployed; second, the slowing up of technological improvement will inevitably retard the development of a richer economy which alone can serve as the base for a real prosperity.

The proponents of the purchasing-power theory meet both of these arguments head on. The capital resources of America are today, they assert, sufficient to give us a degree of prosperity never before known in the history of the world. The problem is not that of developing greater and still greater capital resources for future generations to enjoy, but to make effective use of the capital resources we have. The problem is to set the wheels of industry going now, not in the year 2034. Although they concede that the slowing up of savings will bring a decrease in industrial construction and thus keep out of work a number of people who in the boom period have been employed, they nevertheless insist that for everyone thus kept out of employment in the heavy industries, two, three, or four will be employed elsewhere. They insist that the national income is not a static thing, but something having two component parts, volume and velocity. Money spent by the consumer, they insist, moves with much greater velocity than that disbursed by the investor. A laborer's quarter spent for a can of tomatoes goes first to the retailer, then to the wholesaler, then to the manufacturer or canner, then to the farmer, then, in part at least, back to the retailer, and in part to the maker of farm machinery.

Still another line of attack upon the purchasing-power theory comes from those who insist that the raising of wages and shortening of hours is simply imposing upon American industry additional costs which make it more and more difficult for our industrialists to compete in international trade. We simply cannot undersell Europe. Hence the present policy of increasing wages is simply preventing the return to employment of the thousands who have been in the past, and might well be in the future, supplying the needs of world trade.

Although this likewise is conceded by the proponents of the theory, they insist that in the first place the tremendous drive for self-sufficiency in Europe had already eliminated most of our foreign market, and second that the increased human efficiency due to shortening of hours, together with the rapidly increasing technological improvement of American industry, will more than offset the increased wages and shortened hours imposed by the codes, if and when the barriers to international trade are finally removed.

Whether the purchasing-power theory has sufficient validity to justify the legislative program which has been postulated upon it, we shall in due course know.

CHAPTER TWENTY-FIVE

THE DILEMMA OF THE CONSUMER

A SECOND problem which has been accentuated in the American economic order by the National Industrial Recovery Act is the problem of the consumer.

Can no way be found to stop the fall in prices? Is there no way to eliminate cut-throat competition? These were the questions which were on the tongues of thousands of business men throughout the country as the depression ran its course. And, without question, one of the chief reasons the business community has supported the National Recovery Administration thus far is because it sees in the recovery program possibilities of price stability unattainable under the anti-trust laws.

The price-control devices which have been written into the codes vary from industry to industry.[1] For the most part they fall into four categories: those establishing minimum prices; those prohibiting the selling of commodities below the cost of production; those establishing open-price arrangements of one sort or another; and those designed to limit production.

At least six different formulæ are to found. In some of the codes provision is made for minimum prices which "shall be fair and reasonable"; in others, it is stipulated

[1] This analysis rests in large measure upon George Terborgh's, *Price Control Devices in N.R.A. Codes,* Brookings Institution, Washington, D. C. 1934.

"they shall be equal to the 'lowest reasonable cost of production.'" In still other codes, minimum prices are to equal "the cost of the 'lowest representative firm'"; and in still others, these prices are to be "compensatory."

One need not be a master of rhetoric to realize that these phrases in fact mean nothing.

A little more specific are two other provisions which frequently appear in the codes. "Minimum prices shall equal the 'weighted average cost' of production"; "minimum mark-ups shall equal the 'modal' cost of handling and selling." Here at least are two mathematical formulæ on the basis of which accountants can direct their efforts in the calculation of minimum prices.

One cannot help but wonder, however, whether it will be at all possible to formulate a system of minimum prices on any grounds other than those of expediency, and—more important—whether it will be possible to enforce a system of minimum prices once it has been established.

A second provision common to many codes is that which prohibits the selling of an article below the cost of production. The cost of production referred to is in most cases the cost to each individual firm. If this provision is to be taken at its face value it automatically eliminates from the business community all firms whose costs of production "exceed the current market price." The enforcement of such a provision would obviously cause a price rise of an exceedingly dramatic character and create an unemployment situation of no small magnitude, not to mention the aggravation of the problem of law enforcement beyond anything with which the government can at present hope to cope. To avoid the difficulties inherent in this situation a considerable number of the codes specifically permit a member to sell below cost if it is necessary for him to do so in order to meet his competitors. In fact, all of the codes have been interpreted in a fashion which makes such price-cutting possible.

Just what these provisions, so interpreted, are designed to accomplish is difficult to understand. They do, perhaps, place a limit on price-cutting, at the cost of the lowest producer. In theory the initiative in price-cutting can now come only from those who are facing cut-throat competition, and in theory price-cutting cannot go below the price that the lowest cost producer is able to charge and still make an acceptable profit. In fact, however, the problem of enforcement is inconceivably difficult. One need only mention the complexities involved in setting up a cost-accounting system in those industries in which the items produced run into hundreds, if not thousands, without making any reference to the varied and diverse methods of evasion.

A third technique, which has been extensively used in the codes in an endeavor to introduce price stability, is the establishment of open price systems. Such codes usually "require that within a specified period after the effective date the members of the industry must file with the code authority or some other designated body the prices, discounts, and terms of sale on which they are transacting business. Thereafter, until revisions of these schedules have been duly put into effect, the members are forbidden to carry on business, except in some cases with express permission, at prices or on terms other than those filed." This technique may be useful as a supplementary measure to other forms of price control. Without it the enforcement of the provisions relating to minimum costs or sales below cost of production would be virtually impossible of administration. It may also be used, one might remark, to develop monopolies in those industries in which the other requisite factors for the development of monopolistic conditions are present. How effective it will be in introducing price stability into those industries in which semi-monopolistic conditions do not already exist is exceedingly dubious.

The possibilities of evasion are almost legion. An attempt has been made to forestall such evasions in a number of the codes by characterizing them as unfair trade practices. Among those most frequently mentioned are, "(1) excessive contributions to customers' advertising costs, (2) the purchase of his receivables, (3) the payment of excessive rentals for use of a part of his premises, (4) loans to or endorsements for him, (5) the purchase from him of patents, stocks, or competitive materials or other articles, (6) offering him products not subject to the code at abnormally low prices, (7) the purchase of capital stock or other interest in his business."

A fourth and final method which has been resorted to in an endeavor to introduce price stability into industry is "through control of the supply of goods coming on the market." This technique has had two developments: first, "the allotment of production quotas to individual members of industry"; and second, a "uniform limitation on machine hours."

The problem of anticipating consumption, be it remarked, is in and of itself no easy one, for, in many things at least, consumption is inextricably tied up with the price level. The device consequently may easily become a mere technique for propping up the price level through the curtailment of production.

The inevitable conclusion to which one is seemingly forced is that although in those industries in which cut-throat competition and price instability are serious problems, price fixing, prohibiting selling below cost and open price associations may exercise a beneficial influence for a time, they will, sooner or later, break down. In those industries in which the stage is otherwise set for monopolistic developments they will, in all probability, constitute a definite stimulus to such development. The only really effective technique for the introduction of price stability into industry is control of production. This has, however, very distinct disadvantages, not least among which is the fact that it may very easily become a weapon in the armory of the monopolist.

Thus we are again faced with a dilemma. Price-control mechanisms will prove of little or no value in many industries; in others they may well be effective. Their effectiveness will, with few exceptions, be in direct ratio to the presence of certain other factors conducive to monopolistic developments within a given industry. In so far as those industries are concerned in which these devices may be used effectively, three courses are possible—a retreat to the anti-trust laws, uncontrolled monopoly, government regulation. The second is inconceivable. In consequence, only two courses are possible—a retreat to such protections as the anti-trust laws may afford, or government regulation.

That the Administration is considering retreating to the anti-trust laws is suggested by the presidential order of June 8th, barring price-fixing clauses in the pending codes and the further order of June 29th, permitting bidders for governmental contracts to underbid the established price by as much as 15 per cent.

CHAPTER TWENTY-SIX

STRIKES AND LOCKOUTS

A PART of the National Industrial Recovery machinery, and yet not a part of the National Recovery Administration are the various and sundry labor boards which have been set up.

With "the return of prosperity" and the encouragement given labor under Section 7a of the National Industrial Recovery Act, it was almost inevitable that labor disputes should become more and more acute as time went by. In an endeavor to supplement the work of the Conciliation Service of the Department of Labor, there was established the National Labor Board, under which some twenty or more regional boards have been created. More recently, additional boards of a similar character have been appointed in connection with certain code authorities under the National Recovery Administration.

By and large the National Labor Board and its subsidiaries have done a reasonably effective job in settling or postponing many of the strikes which have threatened to tear industry apart. Nevertheless, the jurisdiction of the National Labor Board, and its authority to make a definitive interpretation of the law, has been challenged more than once. The feeling developed, consequently, that a statutory definition of the authority of these various labor boards was imperative.

Although the attempt to pass the Wagner bill failed,

the Labor Disputes Joint Resolution, a compromise measure was adopted. Briefly summarized, the Resolution authorized the President "to establish a board, or boards, to investigate issues, facts, practices, and activities of employers or employes in controversies arising under Section 7a of the National Industrial Recovery Act or which are burdening or obstructing, or threatening to burden or obstruct, the free flow of interstate commerce." It empowered any board so established to conduct an election by secret ballot among employes to determine by what person, persons, or organizations they wanted to be represented. Thus an effort is being made to insure the right of employes to organize and to select representatives for the purpose of collective bargaining as defined in Section 7a. The life of the Board is limited to one year, at the end of which time the controversial Wagner bill is again to receive consideration.

Under the provisions of the Resolution the National Labor Relations Board has been established with the full sweep of authority conferred by the Resolution. Whether it will be more successful than its predecessors in adjudicating the various industrial disputes which will of necessity come before it, the year will tell. Needless to say its success or failure will bear a direct relation to the success or failure of the New Deal.

THE HOME-OWNER

CHAPTER TWENTY-SEVEN

SAVING THE HOME-OWNER

By no means as important as the farm relief program, or the National Industrial Recovery Act, nevertheless, not without significance was and is the attempt to save the urban home-owner.

As in the case of agriculture, the continuance of the depression was forcing foreclosure after foreclosure in every city in the land. Through no fault of their own, thousands of hard-working men were losing properties in which they had, in many cases, invested their life savings. Family after family, previously in comfortable circumstances, was finding itself on the street. The psychological effect of the cataclysm upon tens of thousands of our fellow citizens can never be measured. The mental anguish and the suffering of those actually dispossessed, however, were by no means the only consequence of the foreclosures then in progress. The dumping of thousands of pieces of property on the real-estate market in the course of a few months could have but one result—an undue depression of all real-estate values. This, in turn, was forcing into bankruptcy business after business. Even more serious was the fact that these bankruptcies threatened the solvency of hundreds of financial institutions.

The Home-Owners Loan Act was designed, therefore, not only to save the thousands about to be dispossessed, but to relieve the pressure on those businesses and financial institutions whose solvency was threatened. To this end, the Home-Owners Loan Corporation, with a capital of two hundred million dollars, was created. Under its ægis, two billion dollars' worth of 4-per-cent bonds could be issued. These bonds originally were guaranteed by the Federal government only as to interest, although they were tax exempt, both as to principal and interest—except for estate, inheritance, gift, and surtaxes. The condition of the money market has been such, however, that Congress has recently decided to guarantee the principal as well and, incidentally to increase the total to which such bonds may be issued to $3,000,000,000.

It was obviously impossible for the government to take over the twenty billion dollars' worth of mortgages on real estate throughout the country. The scope of the Home-Owners Loan Act was confined, therefore, to properties worth $20,000 or less where the home-owner, unable to keep up interest and principal payments, was faced with foreclosure. Thus, the most acute cases of distress would be met, and thus, in a measure at least, the pressure upon the real estate market would be relieved.

The authors of the Act were aware of the fact, moreover, that it would be impossible, through a single procedure, to extend relief to the thousands who were in desperate need. Three different methods of disbursing relief were, in consequence, written into the measure. The first involved the mere exchange of the bonds of the Home-Owners Loan Corporation for the outstanding mortgage in all cases in which the mortgagee could be persuaded to accept such an exchange. Under such circumstances, the home-owner could borrow from the Home-Owners Loan Corporation an amount up to 80 per cent of the current appraised value of his property, providing, however, that the sum requested did not exceed $14,000. In connection with the exchange of such mortgages, incidentally, the Corporation was empowered to advance such cash as might be necessary to pay back taxes and assessments, provided the total amount borrowed did not exceed the 80-per-cent limit. These loans bear 5 per cent interest, and are to be repaid over a period of fifteen years. Amortization payments are made annually, semi-annually, quarterly, or monthly, as circumstances dictate. A period of grace of not more than three years may be permitted at any time, if the Corporation decided that "circumstances of the home-owner and the condition of the security justify such an extension."

So slight is the variation in procedure involved when the exchange of bonds is for the purpose of redeeming or recovering homes already lost through foreclosure that it scarcely deserves mention.

In the event that the mortgagee refuses to accept the bonds of the Home-Owners Loan Corporation and the mortgages, taxes, and other incumbrances on the property do not exceed 40 per cent of its appraised value, the owner may apply for a cash advance with which to take up the mortgage. Such an advance is made, however, only if the home-owner is in imminent danger of foreclosure and a loan from the ordinary lending agencies cannot be obtained. Loans of this character bear 6 per cent interest.

Should any cases arise in which a home-owner is faced with the loss of his property because of non-payments of back taxes, or assessments, or because of the imperative necessity of making repairs, the Home-Owners Loan Corporation may make an advance of cash up to 50 per cent of the value of the property, provided the property is not otherwise incumbered. Loans of this character are to bear an interest charge of 5 per cent.

The Home-Owners Loan Corporation—the administrative agency set up for the purpose of carrying out the provisions of the Home-Owners Loan Act—is, in a sense, a subsidiary agency of the Federal Home Loan Bank Board, the members of which act as the board of directors of the Corporation. A Washington office, consisting of a general manager, a general counsel, a treasurer and their staffs, has been established. Headquarters have been opened in each of the forty-eight states and in Hawaii. Branch offices have been set up wherever the pressure of business has necessitated their establishment. There now are nearly 300 state and branch offices, employing about 12,000 persons. The organization at the moment includes a title examiner and appraisers in almost every county in the United States.

Once an application has been filed it is analyzed by the state manager or his assistants, and the applicant is interviewed. A considerable number of applications are rejected at this stage of the proceedings. It may be that the property is not a home. It may very quickly appear that it is worth more than $20,000. Or it may be that the home-owner is not in distress, but is trying to chisel 1 per cent off the interest he is now paying. Many persons have sought to take unjustifiable advantage of the Act.

If the application falls within the provisions of the Act, a preliminary appraisal is made. This may reveal that the property is in reality worth more than $20,000, or it may show that the owner's equity is so small that it has already been wiped out or so small that it would be impossible to extend the requested relief.

Should this early appraisal reveal that the property is such that a loan can be made, an administrative officer of the Corporation communicates with the mortgagee and others who may have interest in the property in an endeavor to discover whether some method of refinancing other than through a loan from the Corporation can be arranged. If this proves to be impossible, the Corporation agent then attempts to obtain the mortgagees consent to an exchange of Home-Owners Loan Corporation bonds for the mortgage.

Should the mortgagee refuse to accept the bonds in exchange for his mortgage, the possibility of relieving the owner's distress through a cash loan of not more than 40 per cent of the appraised value of the property is considered. Such a loan is possible, however, only where the mortgage is small—not exceeding $8,000. If the mortgage represents 60 or 70 per cent of the appraised value of the property, the application must be rejected. If, however, the mortgagee gives his consent to an exchange of bonds, or if a 40-per-cent cash loan appears to be adequate, a detailed appraisal of the property is made. Should it become evident that the property is in imperative need of repairs, bids for such repairs may be obtained. In calculating the total amount of the loan needed, the cost of such necessary repairs will be included in the computation.

An investigation is also made into the character of the applicant. If both the detailed appraisal and the character report prove satisfactory, the title is searched.

If the title proves satisfactory, the state manager, or

his assistant, may close the loan. All cash loans are subject to approval of the Corporation directors in Washington. This is the routine which must be followed in connection with each application for a loan from the Home-Owners Loan Corporation.

On April 27, 1934, the Home-Owners Loan Act was, as I have already indicated, amended to permit the issuance of bonds guaranteed as to principal as well as interest. In consequence of this action the Corporation has been able to reduce its interest rate from 4 per cent to 3 per cent; more important, perhaps, the exchange of bonds for mortgages has been definitely expedited.

Despite certain difficulties connected with organization and personnel, the Corporation has made very satisfactory progress. The recipient of 1,510,307 applications for loans totaling more than $4,856,269,830, the staff of the Corporation has checked practically all of them and made a detailed appraisal of almost 1,000,000. Down to August 10th, the Corporation had saved approximately 447,848 homes from foreclosure and disbursed a total of over $1,346,382,489. In addition, the Corporation is closing loans at the rate of 14,000 to 15,000 a week.

Whether or not the Home-Owners Loan Corporation has pegged the price level of urban real estate at the point it had reached when the measure was enacted into law, it has without question relieved the pressure on urban real estate tremendously.

TRANSPORTATION AND COMMUNICATION

CHAPTER TWENTY-EIGHT

TRANSPORTATION AND COMMUNICATION

LESS significant still than the National Industrial Recovery Act, or the Agricultural Adjustment Act, but nevertheless not without some importance, is the Emergency Railroad Transportation Act. The Act is obviously designed for three purposes: the prevention of unnecessary failures among our transportation units, the tightening up of the control the Interstate Commerce Commission exercises over transportation agencies, and the introduction of economies of such a character as to benefit not only those holding railroad equities, but the general public as well.

The desirability of preventing the unnecessary collapse of any of the larger units in our economic system is obvious. The failure of a great railroad system might easily lead to a shattering of the confidence the recovery program has been slowly building. Equally obvious is it, however, that the perpetuation in our transportation system of a capital structure which is fundamentally unsound is merely postponing the inevitable, and bolstering a weakness in our financial system which will sooner or later lead to collapse.

To prevent a repetition of the railroad scandals which characterized the decade preceding 1929, the authority of the Interstate Commerce Commission has been extended to "corporations controlling railroads but not themselves carriers." No less important, however, were the amendments to the Interstate Commerce Act repealing the "recapture clause" and facilitating mergers and consolidations.

Somewhat more unique were the provisions establishing a Federal Coordinator of Transport, whose duty it was and is (1) "to encourage and promote or require action on the part of the carriers and of subsidiaries subject to the Interstate Commerce Act as amended which will (a) avoid unnecessary duplication of services and facilities of whatever nature and permit the joint use of terminals and truckage incident thereto or requisite to such joint use: Provided that no routes now existing shall be eliminated except with the consent of all participating lines or upon the order of the Coordinator; (b) control allowances, accessorial services and the charges therefore, and other practices affecting service or operation, to the end that undue impairment of net earnings may be prevented; and (c) avoid other wastes, and preventable expense; (2) to promote financial reorganization of the carriers, with due regard to legal rights, so as to reduce fixed charges to the extent required by the public interest and improve carrier credit: and (3) to provide for the immediate study of other means of improving conditions surrounding transportation in all its forms and the preparation of plans therefore."

For the accomplishment of these objectives both a Washington office and a field staff have been improvised. The Washington office has been divided into six sections: Legislative Research, Transportation Service, Car Pooling, Purchases, Labor, and Cost-finding.

The work of the section on Legislative Research has been confined to a study of those matters relative to which there is an obvious need of additional legislation. Most significant among these needs are railroad consolidation, the regulation of transportation agencies other than railroads, and certain minor amendments to the existing laws.

The section on Transportation is at the moment in the middle of four major surveys dealing with merchandise traffic, passenger traffic, car-loading and marketing. Some idea of the comprehensive character of the merchandising survey may be obtained from the fact that not only is an appraisal of the value of merchandising and its distribution among the several competing agencies being made, but an analysis of the service requirements of the traffic, and the charges which the traffic can and should bear, has been undertaken. In addition, a study of the relative economic capacity (present and potential) from a cost-and-service standpoint, of the several competing transportation agencies, and the formulation of a plan which will coordinate each of these agencies to the extent of the greatest economic utility, are in progress.

No less widespread are the ramifications of the passenger-traffic survey, encompassing as it does the determination of the causes of the increasing loss of passenger traffic by the railroads, the ascertainment of the relative efficiency from both service and economic standpoints of the various passenger-carrying agencies, a measuring of the potential markets for railway passenger service, an investigation into the means by which railroad passenger service may be more economically operated so that charges to patrons may be lowered accordingly, and the devising of methods by which the various passenger agencies can be operated both more economically and more efficiently.

The section on Car Pooling is chiefly concerned with the more effective use of existing equipment; that on

Purchasing, with the introduction of economies through the standardization of equipment; the improvement of purchasing methods generally, and the encouragement of scientific research.

Although the Coordinator has deemed it his duty to see that section 7e of the Act covering the relation of railroads to the unionization of their employes has been called to the attention of the managements, the chief function of the section on Labor has been the collection of information relative to the possibility of reducing the length of the working-day, week and month, the desirability of a dismissal wage, pensions, unemployment benefits, a specialized placement service for railroad employes, the merging of seniority rosters in future mergers or consolidations, and the indemnification of employes for property losses and personal expense in connection with transfer.

One should perhaps include here the fact that the Act itself specifically provides that "the number of employes in the service of a carrier shall not be reduced by reason of any action taken pursuant to the authority of this title below the number as shown by the payrolls of employes in service during the month of May, 1933, after deducting the number who have been removed from the payrolls after the effective date of this Act by reason of death, normal retirements, or resignation, but not more in any one year than 5 per cent of said number in service during May, 1933." Needless to say this provision makes impossible any radical reorganization of railroad management as it affects labor.

The cost-finding section is engaged in an analysis of the unit cost of the services rendered. Through a comparison and contrast of the various railways it is hoped that at least the grossest inefficiencies of railway management may thus be revealed.

In addition to the Washington office the Federal Coordinator has set up, pursuant to the provisions of the law, three regional coordinating committees; one for the Eastern group of railways; one for the South, and one for the West. Each of these committees is made up of five regular and two special members, the latter representing the so-called "short-line," and the electric lines respectively. A regional director personally responsible to the Coordinator works with each of these regional committees. The committees have charge, for the most part, of investigations into operating and management economies local to each region, such as the unification of terminal facilities, the joint use of shops, etc. As a result of these studies the Coordinator hopes to be able to make such recommendations relative to the improvement of railroad service as will not only restore the railroads to a self-sustaining basis, but will also confer considerable benefits upon the public.

Down to date the Federal Coordinator of Transportation has, pursuant to law, made two reports to Congress —one relating to "the need for a radical or major change in the organization, conduct, and regulations of the railroad industry which can be accomplished by Federal legislation"; the other relating to the regulation of transportation agencies other than railroads.

The first of these reports, after a detailed analysis of the various ills of railroad organization and administration, came to the conclusion that government ownership and unification would, from a purely technical point of view, most satisfactorily solve the problem. Nevertheless, because of the exigencies of politics, it seemed to the Federal Coordinator unwise to recommend such a radical reorganization of our system of transport at the present time.

The second report concluded that it had become evident that the entire transportation industry, including other agencies as well as the railroads, is in need of the guiding hand of government control, if threatening chaos is to be transformed into order. The Coordinator of Transportation, accordingly, recommended the enactment of measures which could bring both water and motor transport under Federal regulation.

In addition to launching these studies and making these recommendations, the Coordinator participated in the railroad wage settlement of 1933, and was in large measure responsible for the overhauling of the salaries of railway executives, and, more important, in forcing a reduction in the price of steel rails from $40 to $36.375 a ton.

As these various studies progress, further action and further recommendations for legislative action are to be anticipated.

No less important than any of the bills recommended by the Federal Coordinator of Transport, however, was the Railroad Retirement Act, passed without his recommendation. This bill definitely stipulates that each employe, upon having attained the age of sixty-five or having completed 30 years service with a railroad shall receive an annuity, beginning not more than sixty days from the date of his application. The annuity is to be calculated by multiplying the number of years of service up to thirty by 2 per cent of the first $50 of the annuitant's previous compensation, by multiplying by 1-1/2 per cent the next $100 of his compensation, and by 1 per cent the next $150. Any compensation which has been received in excess of $300 is not to enter the computations.

By a written agreement between the employe and the carrier the period of service may be extended up to the age of seventy, but under no circumstances beyond that age limit.

By virtue of this retirement system it is estimated that some 100,000 vacancies will be created in the railway systems in the course of the next year. In consequence it will be possible for the railroads to effect economies hitherto impossible. And, equally important, they will be able despite these economies, to provide employment for a good many thousand men heretofore without it.[1]

No less significant, perhaps, is the grant of power which has just been made to the newly created Federal Communications Commission. In its hands have been concentrated not only the powers previously exercised over radio by the Radio Commission, but also the powers over telephonic and telegraphic communications hitherto exercised by the Interstate Commerce Commission as well. Television and the transoceanic cables similarly fall within its province. To say that it has been given a sweep of authority over these channels of communication commensurate with the authority of the Interstate Com-

[1] Passing mention should perhaps also be made of the air-mail episode. As a result of the air-mail exposures, the President was authorized to appoint a commission for the purpose of making an immediate investigation into every phase of the problem of aviation. A report, carrying with it such recommendations as the commission may see fit to make, is expected by Congress not later than February 1, 1935.

merce Commission over railroad transportation is in no way to magnify its importance. At the direction of the President, it may, in time of war, take over these lines of communication entirely.

WATER POWER

CHAPTER TWENTY-NINE

THE TENNESSEE VALLEY AUTHORITY

NOT the least interesting of the projects of the Recovery Program is that embodied in the Tennessee Valley Authority Act designed "to improve the navigability and to provide for the flood control of the Tennessee River; to provide for reforestation, and proper use of marginal lands in the Tennessee Valley; to provide for the agricultural and industrial development of the said valley; to provide for the national defense by the creation of a corporation for the operating of the government properties, at and near Muscle Shoals in the State of Alabama, and for other purposes."

To carry out the purpose of the Act, the Tennessee Valley Authority was incorporated, under a board of three directors appointed by the President, with a capitalization of $50,000,000 and authority to issue bonds upon the credit of the United States, up to a total of not more than $50,000,000 more. These bonds are to bear interest incidentally at not more than 3½ per cent. Such income as may come from the sale of electricity or nitrate, moreover, is to become the property of the corporation.

As the directors of the Tennessee Valley Authority have understood the mandate imposed upon them, the T.V.A. has eleven major objectives. Briefly summarized these may be said to be: "first, a new deal for the residents of the Tennessee Valley; second, the development of methods of regional planning; third, the improvement of agriculture and the proper utilization of marginal lands; fourth, the development of domestic industries to supplement agriculture in providing local employment; fifth, the utilization of Muscle Shoals as a yardstick in the determination of the relative costs of public and private power operations; sixth, the distribution of its power to the greatest number of people at the lowest possible cost and the conservation of it as an asset of national defense; seventh, the production of cheap fertilizer, and fertilizer materials; eighth, the opening of the Tennessee River to an economic maximum of navigation; ninth, the development of the maximum flood control; tenth, the promotion of reforestation and methods of retarding soil erosion; and eleventh, the conservation and utilization of the basic mineral and other natural resources."

Down to date the Authority has concentrated its efforts upon developing the power projects as the speediest way of accomplishing the larger number of its objectives. The Wilson Dam had already been completed at the time the T.V.A. took over the Muscle Shoals properties. Work was immediately started, however, not only upon the $34,000,000 Norris dam designed both for the production of electricity and for the control of floods on the Tennessee, but also upon the $15,000,000 Wheeler Dam. In this fashion, incidentally, the T.V.A. has been contributing its bit to the tremendous program of government spending which we shall discuss later.

Concomitantly with the start of construction work at the Norris and Wheeler dams, the T.V.A. launched on its power program—designed to revolutionize the Tennessee Valley—and incidentally to serve as a yardstick by which the relative efficiency of public and private utilities might be measured.

As early as August 25, 1933, the T.V.A. set forth its power policy. It asserted that

(1) The business of generating and distributing electric power is a public business.

(2) Private and public interests in the business of power are of different kind and quality and should not be confused.

(3) The interest of the public in the widest possible use of power is superior to any private interest. (Where the private interest and this public interest conflict, the public interest must prevail.)

(4) Where there is a conflict between public interest and private interest in power which can be reconciled without injury to the public interest, such reconciliation should be made.

(5) The right of a community to own and operate its own electric plant is undeniable. (This is one of the measures which the people may properly take to protect themselves against unreasonable rates. Such a course of action may take the form of acquiring the existing plant or setting up a competing plant, as circumstances may dictate.)

(6) The fact that action by the Authority may have an adverse economic effect upon a privately owned utility should be a matter for the serious consideration of the Board in framing and executing its power program. But it is not the determining factor. The most important considerations are the furthering of the public interest in making power available at the lowest rate consistent with sound financial policy, and the accomplishment of the social objectives which low-cost power makes possible. The Authority cannot decline to take action solely upon the ground that to do so would injure a privately owned utility.

(7) To provide a workable and economic basis of opera-

tions, the Authority plans initially to serve certain definite regions and to develop its program in those areas before going outside.

(8) The initial areas selected by the Authority may be roughly described as:

(a) The region immediately proximate to the route of the transmission line soon to be constructed by the Authority between Muscle Shoals and the site of Norris Dam.

(b) The region in proximity to Muscle Shoals, including northern Alabama and northeastern Mississippi.

(c) The region in the proximity of Norris Dam (the new source of power to be constructed by the Authority on the Clinch River in northeast Tennessee).

At a later stage in the development it is contemplated to include, roughly, the drainage area of the Tennessee River in Kentucky, Alabama, Georgia and North Carolina and in that part of Tennessee which lies east of the west margin of the Tennessee drainage area. To make the area a workable one and a fair measure of public ownership, it should include several cities of substantial size (such as Chattanooga and Knoxville) and, ultimately, at least one city of more than a quarter million, within transmission distance, such as Birmingham, Memphis, Atlanta, or Louisville.

While it is the Authority's present intention to develop its power program in the above-described territory before considering going outside, the Authority may go outside the area if there are substantial changes in general conditions, facts, or government policy, which would necessarily require a change in this policy of regional development, or if the privately owned utilities in the area do not cooperate in the working out of the program.

Nothing in the procedure here adopted is to be construed in any sense a commitment against extending the Authority's power operations outside the areas selected, if the above conditions or the public interest requires. Where special considerations exist, justifying the Authority going outside this initial area, the Authority will receive and consider applications based on such special considerations. Among such special considerations would be unreasonably high rates for service and a failure or absence of public regulation to protect the public interest.

(9) Every effort will be made by the Authority to avoid the construction of duplicate physical facilities or wasteful competitive practices. Accordingly, where existing lines of privately owned utilities are required to accomplish the Authority's objectives, as outlined above, a genuine effort will be made to purchase such facilities from the private utilities on an equitable basis.

(10) Accounting should show detail of costs and permit of comparison of operations with privately owned plants, to supply a yardstick and an incentive to both private and public managers.

(11) The accounts and records of the Authority as they pertain to power will always be open to inspection by the public.[1]

A twelfth point in the T.V.A.'s power policy is imposed by law, for although the T.V.A. is authorized to sell surplus power "to states, counties, municipalities, corporations, partnerships, or individuals," it is directed to give preference to "states, counties, municipalities, and corporative organizations of citizens or farmers, not organized or doing business for a profit, but primarily organized for the purpose of supplying electricity to its own citizens or members."

In keeping with the broad outlines of policy thus laid down, contracts were drawn which permit or rather require the resale of electricity at remarkably low rates. For the domestic uses the charge is now 3 cents per kilo-

[1] *Survey Graphic,* March, 1934, p. 110.

watt hour for the first 50 kilowatt hours; 2 cents per kilowatt hour for the next 150; 1 cent per kilowatt hour for the next 200; and .4 cents per kilowatt hour for all over that amount. In consequence electric bills in the municipalities which are now receiving electrical energy from the T.V.A. have been cut in some cases by as much as 50 per cent. Needless to say, similar reductions in the cost of power for commercial purposes have also been made possible.[2]

Thus the first step in the electrification of the Tennessee Valley has been or is in the process of being taken. And at the same time the foundation has been laid, on the basis of which a radical reorganization of the economic life of the Tennessee Valley is rendered possible.

As the directors of the T.V.A. see it, however, a low electrical rate is only half the battle. As long as electrical appliances continue to sell at prohibitive rates the current simply will not be used at any price. In consequence the Electrical Home and Farm Corporation, a subsidiary of the T.V.A., was formed with a capital of $1,000,000 allotted from the Public Works Fund. With the aid of an additional $10,000,000, already ear-marked by the Reconstruction Finance Corporation it plans a campaign, already begun, for the more extensive use of electrical equipment in the homes and on the farms throughout the Tennessee Valley. It hopes to accomplish its objective partially through an educational campaign, but to a larger degree through reducing the cost of elec-

[2] Mention should perhaps be made here of a Congressional Resolution passed April 14, 1934, which directed the Federal Power Commission to investigate and compile the rates charged for electrical energy and its service to residential, rural, commercial, and industrial consumption throughout the United States by private and municipal corporations. What information the report will contain, what use will be made of the information it does contain, yet remains to be seen.

trical equipment and through financing consumer purchases.

Through an agreement with a number of the leading manufacturers of electrical appliances throughout the country, standard equipment designed in part at least by the T.V.A. is now being manufactured for sale at prices 25 per cent to 30 per cent below previous quotations. Thus the instrument is being forged which is to transfer the whole economic life of the Valley.

In addition to the development of electrical energy, plans are being laid, and activities undertaken, which, although by no means as momentous as the electrification of the Valley are by no means insignificant. Not least among these are the building and operation of the nitrate plants at Muscle Shoals, the attempts which are being made to prevent erosion, the steps which are being taken for future reforestation, the model communities which are being erected for the workers, and the vocational training given to the workers on the various construction projects.

Nevertheless, the fact is that down to date the rapid progress which has been made in the electrification of the Valley is the most significant aspect of the work of the T.V.A. What the future will bring in the way of a balanced economy within the region affected still remains to be seen.

RELIEF AND PUBLIC WORKS

CHAPTER THIRTY

PUBLIC RELIEF

On May 22, 1933, when the Federal Emergency Relief Administration was established, some 4,250,000 families, totaling nearly 19,000,000 persons, were receiving relief from public funds. So great was the strain, state and local resources were simply cracking. What the consequences would have been had the Federal government not taken action it is today difficult to conceive.

To meet the emergency, Congress made available some $500,000,000 to be expended through the states as a means of cooperating with them in meeting the needs of the unemployed. This fund was divided into two parts. The first $250,000,000 was made available to the states on the basis of one dollar for each three dollars of public money spent in the states for unemployment relief during the preceding three months. The second $250,000,000 was to be distributed at the discretion of the Administration to those states whose relief needs were so great and whose financial resources were so depleted that additional assistance was needed.

The Federal Emergency Relief Administration at once notified the states that they must not expect the Federal government to finance more than a reasonable proportion of the total. Through the insistence of the Federal Administration, the amount appropriated by the states was increased from an average of $9,914,000 a month during the spring of 1933 to $14,516,000 in October. As the depression wore on, however, the requirement for matching funds had to be waived more and more frequently.

At the head of the Federal Emergency Relief Administration is the Federal Administrator, Harry Hopkins. Under him are the heads of special divisions, the research and statistical experts, the field examiners, who review the accounts of each state administration, and a staff of seven field representatives, who are constantly in touch with each state administration.

A somewhat similar set-up is found in each of the state emergency relief administrations. In the local emergency relief administrations, however, there are, in addition to the necessary administrative personnel, trained workers who investigate the needs of applicants for relief and see that only those in actual want are assisted.

Although direct relief was, of necessity, resorted to in the very beginning, a serious effort was made to substitute work relief wherever possible, with the result that by November 1st, some 2,000,000 people were on work relief rather than on direct relief. In this way an attempt was made to preserve the self-respect of the recipients of relief. In some cases, where the projects upon which the recipients of this relief worked were obviously worth while, this objective was undoubtedly attained. In other cases, where the work was obviously of a trumped-up character, it is dubious whether the differentiation between the two kinds of relief amounted to much.

Despite the assistance thus rendered by the Federal government (and the Federal government be it said, parenthetically, supplied 75 per cent or more of the total funds for relief purposes) the aid actually extended was far from munificent. In May, 1933, $15.59 was the grand total actually given an average family dependent upon public relief for subsistence. By November, however, the amount had been increased to $18.22, although the amount given varied from state to state. Three dollars and eighty-six cents a month was Mississippi's niggardly dole. Compared with this, New York's $43.77 seems almost magnificent. Nevertheless, when one remembers that these figures represent the total income on which four people were expected to live, obtaining therewith food, clothing, shelter, fuel, light, household necessities, and medical care, few there are who will accuse the relief agencies of extravagance.

In addition to the monetary relief thus extended, the Federal Surplus Relief Corporation, to which reference has already been made, purchased and distributed some 89,826,868 pounds of salt pork, some 8,646,500 pounds of smoked pork, 38,443,575 pounds of flour, 5,991,610 pounds of butter, 4,129,660 pounds of beans, 680,243 bushels of wheat, and 983,664 bushels of corn. Even so, the charge of extravagance can hardly be made.

Indeed, one cannot help wondering how soon the ravages of under-nourishment, which have been inevitable under the circumstances, will begin to be recorded in the vital statistics.

Partly because of the inadequacy of the relief appropriation, partly because relief, even though administered with the best intentions, undermines the morale of its recipients, and partly because the public-works program had not progressed as rapidly as had been hoped, the Civil Works program was launched with $400,000,000 allocated to it from the Public Works fund. Of the 3,000,000 men and women on the relief rolls October 30th, 2,000,000 were to be transferred to Civil Works—and some 2,000,000 more of the unemployed provided with employment—a total of 4,000,000 all told.

The administration of the Civil Works program was put under the Federal Emergency Relief Administrator. The state and local administrative organizations set up were for the most part, the previously existing relief organizations.

All persons on work-relief rolls on November 20, 1933, were transferred to the payrolls of the Civil Works Administration, and on the first pay day some 1,100,000 workers received C.W.A. checks. By January 18, 1934, the number of those so employed had risen to 4,040,000. Federal Emergency Relief projects already under way were turned over to the Civil Works Administration, and new projects originating in the Federal Administration, in the states and in the political subsidiaries thereof, were added.

These projects, for the most part, fell into definite categories—streets, roads and highways; schools and universities; parks and playgrounds; public buildings and equipment; improvement to public land; pest control; sanitation; waterways and water supply; utilities; administration, professional and clerical.

The work in connection with roadways and highways was varied in character, including grading, paving, resurfacing, building and replacing ditches, culverts, etc.; laying sidewalks, landscaping, painting and installing street signs. Equally diverse was the work under the other categories.

A thirty-hour week and an eight-hour day were established as a maximum work week for employes doing manual work, and a thirty-nine-hour week for clerical and professional workers. The wage scale of the Federal Administration of Public Works for manual workers was adopted. Clerical, office, statistical survey, and professional workers were to be paid the prevailing wage of the community. Minimum rates were established, however, ranging from twelve dollars a week for unskilled clerical workers in the South to forty-five dollars a week for professional workers in the North.

A sample study of the Civil Works Administration reveals the fact that the bulk of the C.W.A. employes received from fifty to fifty-nine cents an hour; 43.8 per cent of all the employes falling into this category; 27.4 per cent receiving from forty to forty-nine cents an hour; and 11.3 per cent, thirty to thirty-nine cents an hour. Thus 80 per cent of the workers on the C.W.A. received less than sixty cents an hour. The number of those receiving a dollar an hour or better constituted only 4.2 per cent of the entire group. Thus, however heavy the burden of the C.W.A. may have been on the public treasury, few of its critics would themselves care to live on the wages paid its employes. One of the consequences of the establishment of the Civil Works Administration was a lightening of the load the Federal Emergency Relief Administration had to bear. The number of those who remained on the relief rolls fell from 3,358,996 families in November to 2,625,870 in December, 1933. And by January 30, 1934, the number had fallen still farther to 2,485,000. With the gradual liquidation of the Civil Works Administration, however, the figure rose in February to 2,630,000 and in March to something over 3,000,000.

By February 1, 1934, more than $437,901,000 had been paid out in wages to C.W.A. workers. An additional appropriation of $950,000,000 was made by Congress on February 15th, for the carrying out of the purpose of the Federal Emergency Relief Act and continuing the C.W.A. —thus bringing the sum total appropriated for relief by the Federal government since the beginning of the depression to $2,150,000,000.[1]

By April 2nd less than 100,000 persons were left on the Civil Works Administration's rolls. They were, for the most part, connected with the administrative aspects of the organization, or were completing certain minor projects.

The reason for the liquidation of the C.W.A. was the desire of the Federal Emergency Relief Administrator to launch an emergency work program definitely limited to persons established as being actually in need of relief. The character of the work was not to be changed, but the administration thereof was to be definitely tightened up.

The obvious necessity of carrying on relief through 1934-35 caused the second session of the seventy-third Congress to appropriate another $525,000,000 for relief purposes. A large portion of this sum has already been ear-marked for the drought regions.

Subsidiary in part to the Federal Emergency Relief Administration and in part to the Agricultural Adjustment Administration is the Federal Surplus Relief Corporation to which reference has already been made. Established for the twofold purpose of agricultural and unemployment relief through the purchase of certain agricultural commodities and the distribution thereof to the

[1] Three hundred millions of this amount, be it said, incidentally, was appropriated during the Hoover administration.

unemployed, it had, down to March 31, 1934, the last date for which figures are available, purchased and distributed agricultural commodities with an estimated value of $58,000,000.

Closely allied to these activities, yet distinct therefrom, is the work of the Civilian Conservation Corps. Through it in the course of the last eighteen months some 600,000 young men have been taken off the streets and out of the ranks of the unemployed, and, equally important, a substantial contribution has been made toward the preservation of the nation's natural resources.

The organization of such a corps was first broached by Mr. Roosevelt in a message to Congress some two weeks after his inauguration. Two weeks later a law authorizing the organization of the Civilian Conservation Corps was passed, and $1,000,000,000 appropriated for its maintenance.

Responsibility for whipping this civilian army into shape was divided among four departments. The Department of Labor assumed responsibility for the selection of the men; the Department of War for their enrollment, equipment, transportation, housing, and care; and the Department of Agriculture and the Interior, for the work in the forests. Nevertheless, so effective was the coordination of the efforts of these departments, the first Civilian Conservation Corps camp was established two weeks after the passage of the Act, and by July 1st the Corps had reached its full strength. Three hundred and ten thousand young men had been enrolled.

As the reader will recall, the Act establishing the Civilian Conservation Corps was passed for the purpose of providing employment for young men. The age limit for membership was limited, consequently, with certain exceptions, to those between the ages of eighteen and twenty-five. A preference is given to those with dependents.

All of the men receive a cash allowance of thirty dollars a month in addition to their board, clothing, shelter, and medical care. The assistant leaders, approximately 8 per cent of the enrollment, receive thirty-six dollars a month, and the leaders, constituting at no time more than 5 per cent of the corps, receive forty-five dollars a month. Of this allowance at least twenty-five dollars a month is sent home to support dependents. Thus the Civilian Conservation Corps provides not only a partial though temporary, solution of the situation in which the youth of the country found itself, but is also a supplementary measure of relief.

The term of enlistment is six months, and although there is no legal contract which compels a man to stay in the Corps, the men are expected to stay their full term. As a matter of fact, at the expiration of the first six months' period 175,000 out of the total 310,000 enrolled in the Corps elected to stay for another six months.

The men have been employed for the most part upon tree and plant disease control, insect-pest control, rodent control, tree-planting, erosion control, forest-stand improvement, the elimination of fire hazard, and the construction of truck trails, telephone lines, and fire breaks.

According to the testimony of experts in the Departments of Interior and of Agriculture they have already advanced the work of forestry by decades.

These, then, in broad outline, are the measures which have been taken by the administration to alleviate the most acute cases of distress caused by the depression.

Equally significant, however, from the point of view of the recovery program is the fact that through these measures between $2,500,000,000 and $3,000,000,000 have been pumped into circulation.

CHAPTER THIRTY-ONE

THE PUBLIC WORKS PROGRAM

No less important than the relief measures is the tremendous appropriation of $3,300,000,000 for public works. In consequence of this appropriation a Federal Emergency Administration of Public Works was created with a Federal Administrator at its head.

Under the supervision of the President, the Administrator was directed to prepare a comprehensive program of public works, including among other things (a) the construction, repair, and improvement of public highways and parkways, public buildings and other publicly-owned instrumentalities and facilities; (b) the conservation and development of natural resources, including the control, utilization and purification of water power, the transmission of electrical energy, and the construction of river and harbor improvements; (c) any projects of a character heretofore constructed or carried on either directly by public authority or with public aid to serve the interests of the general public; (d) the construction, reconstruction, alteration or repair under public regulation or control of low-cost housing and slum-clearance projects; (e) any project of any character heretofore eligible for loans under the provisions of the Emergency Relief and Construction Act of 1932. It was, of course, obviously impossible to await the detailed formulation of a comprehensive plan.

With a view to increasing employment quickly, the

President was authorized and empowered—through the Administrator or through such other agencies as he might designate or create—(1) to construct, finance, or aid in the construction or financing of any public-work projects included in the comprehensive plan referred to above; (2) to make grants to states, municipalities, or other public bodies upon such terms as he, the President, might prescribe for the construction, repair, or improvement of any projects included in the enumeration in the preceding paragraph, but no such grant was to be in excess of 30 per cent of the cost of the labor and the materials employed upon such projects; (3) to acquire by purchase or the power of eminent domain any real or personal property in connection with the construction of any such project; (4) to aid in the financing of such railroad maintenance and equipment as might be approved by the Interstate Commerce Commission; (5) to advance the unappropriated balance of the sum authorized for the construction and equipment of an annex to the Library of Congress.

Thus were the broad outlines of public policy laid down in the Act.

To whip into shape an organization capable of handling the expenditure of $3,300,000,000 was no easy task for the Public Works Administration. Hardly had the National Recovery Act been passed than a Special Board of Public Works was created. On this Board sat Secretary of War Dern, Secretary of Agriculture Wallace, Secretary of Commerce Roper, Secretary of Labor Perkins, Attorney-General Cummings, Director of the Budget Douglas, and the Assistant Secretary of the Treasury. The functions of the Board, as they have developed, have fallen for the most part into three categories; first, advising the President on important matters of public policy, including major appointments to office and major questions of administrative procedure; second, interpreting those portions of the National Industrial Recovery Act which relate to public works; and third, passing on all recommendations for allotments from public-works funds.

Directly in charge of the Public Works Administration is the Administrator, Secretary Ickes. Assisting him directly are a National Planning Board, a Labor Board of Review, a general counsel, two administrative assistants, and a subcommittee on Federal projects.

The functions of the general counsel, the administrative assistants, the Labor Board, and the Office of Investigations are more or less apparent from the titles of these respective agencies. The National Planning Board had as its first assignment the formulation of a comprehensive plan of public works. To date it has been primarily concerned with (1) collecting data on the basis of which it may advise on the proper geographic distribution of public works, (2) the coordination of the activities of the various construction units in the Federal government, (3) the stimulation of city, state, and regional planning, and (4) long-time research. As a matter of fact, events have moved so rapidly that the work of the National Planning Board has not been very effective.

Subordinate to the Administrator in the hierarchy of the Public Works Administration is a Deputy Administrator, who is assisted by four executive assistants and by the Technical Board of Review. He it is who actually exercises the broad powers of general supervision.

Most of the correspondence, as well as the inevitable work of interviewing people, falls on the executive assistants. In so far as possible, the work of the office has been

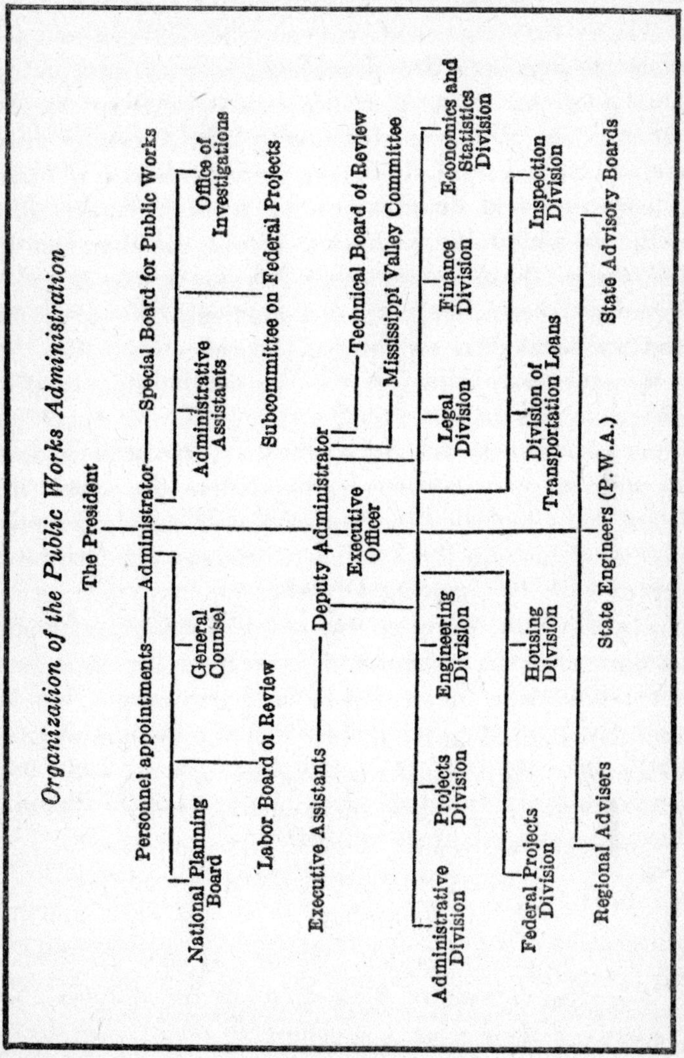

Organization of the Public Works Administration

divided into four categories: general, technical, legal, Civil Works Administration projects and labor questions, each in charge of an executive assistant.

Although the executive officer acts as Deputy Administrator in the absence of his superior, he is for the most part a glorified chief clerk, concerned primarily with the coordination and direction of administrative procedure within the Public Works Administration. As the immediate head of the Administrative Division he is responsible for all purchases, personnel, correspondence, accounting, transportation, and vouchers. The state offices are likewise under his direction, in so far as the routine aspects of their activities are concerned.

Coordinate with the Administrative Division, clearing through the executive officer, but not in the same sense subordinate to him, are the Projects Division (for non-Federal projects), the Legal Division, the Finance Division and the Engineering Division.

The Projects Division was created not only for the purpose of coordinating and expediting the procedure followed by the state administrative organizations, but for the sake of speeding up the work of the three examining divisions—Law, Finance and Engineering—as well. The work of this division has, consequently, been divided into three sections on records, reports, and expedition.

To make certain that all applications for grants or loans fall within the limitations of the Act, the examining divisions have been created. A copy of each application is submitted to each of these divisions for analysis. On the basis of their reports, a composite report is prepared by the Projects Division, and forwarded to the Deputy Administrator. A standardized form of reporting has been worked out for each of these examining divisions. In broad outlines it requires:

1. The corporate name of the applicant, his address, his counsel, his engineer, his architect, and the population of the community involved as given in each of the last three censuses; 2. loan requested, securities offered, period of loan and maturities; 3. loan recommended, type of securities acceptable, period of loan, and tax maturities; 4. engineering considerations, general description, estimate of cost, statement of economic and social value and whether it is part of a long-range program, other planning considerations, statement of all endorsements as well as objections to the project, statement as to competition, as to how soon the project can be started and how many men will be employed; 5. statement as to economic soundness, discussion of the operating income and operating cost and self-liquidating features, with a table of the life of the loan showing amortization and accumulated surplus; 6. financial considerations; legal considerations; conclusions and recommendations which include a definite statement as to the technical and self-liquidating aspects of the project; conditions of the loan which cover conditions the applicant must fulfill and which have to be included in the bond purchase contract.

These reports of the examining divisions are primarily technical in their nature, and make little or no attempt to assess the social desirability of the project under consideration. Should either a state board or one of the examining divisions question the legality or social desirability of any project, the case is turned over to the Technical Board of Review for further consideration.

The Federal Projects Division has as its function the formulation of a Federal program of public works in conjunction with the seventy-three construction agencies of the Federal government. All projects for which Federal funds have been allotted have passed through this division, with the exception of those involving the construction of public buildings. The procedure is usually as follows: (1) A request is made for the allotment of funds by some particular bureau of the Federal government; (2) the request and any substantiating data connected therewith are referred to the Federal Projects Division; (3) the project is examined by the Federal Projects Division from the point of view of the engineering, finance and economics; (4) if the project is approved, the complete file relative thereto is forwarded to a subcommittee on Federal projects of the Special Board of Public Works; (5) upon the completion of its investigation, the subcommittee prepares a report which is presented to the Special Board of Public Works; (6) if this board approves the project, it is submitted to the President for final decision.

The Division of Transportation Loans was set up for handling loans to private carriers for the purchase of new rails and equipment, and for repairs to heavy equipment and for maintenance of way and structures. All such loans must have the approval of the Interstate Commerce Commission. Preliminary correspondence usually precedes the filing of an application until such time as a concrete project possible of serious consideration has been formulated. A tentative application is made, and is then carefully analyzed by the financial and legal examiners of the division and forwarded to the director and assistant general counsel for approval. In the event of their approval, a report is filed with the Administrator. Upon the receipt of his approval, if it is forthcoming, the railroad is notified of the favorable attitude of the Administration.

The Housing Division, as its name implies, deals with all applications for loans on low-cost housing projects. Its work has in large measure been supplanted by the activities of the Federal Public Works Emergency Housing Corporation.

Briefly summarized, the functions of the Division of Economics and Statistics are (1) to assemble, coordinate, analyze and interpret all the general statistics of the Public Works Administration; (2) to coordinate this statistical work with that of other government agencies; (3) to furnish the National Planning Board with such statistical information as that board may require; (4) to represent the Public Works Administration before the Central Statistical Board; and (5) to anticipate the needs of the Deputy Administrator and Administrator for statistical information and analysis.

The Division of Inspection is required to exercise strict supervision over the construction of all non-Federal projects; to see to it that the provisions of the contract entered into are faithfully performed; to see that all the terms and conditions of the plan and specifications are complied with; to see that the codes of fair competition are observed; and to approve payments for work performed.

The work of the Inspection Division, be it said parenthetically, differs from that of the Office of Investigations in that the latter is assigned specific problems for investigation, whereas the former is engaged in routine inspection.

Subordinate to the executive officer, in so far as the administrative aspects of its work are concerned, is the field organization. This organization consists of ten regional advisers, forty-eight state advisory boards, and forty-five state engineers. The regional advisers have as their primary function (1) assisting the National Planning Board in the formulation of a comprehensive plan of public works in each region, (2) stimulating public interest in regional planning, and (3) advising with all Public Work Administration officials within their respective regions.

In each state, moreover, there is a state advisory board to which all non-Federal projects, except housing and transportation loans, must first be submitted. The executive officer of these state advisory boards is the state engineer, who examines each application from a strictly engineering standpoint and makes such recommendations relative to it as he may see fit.

Thus there has evolved in connection with the public works program an elaborate administrative machinery. Through this machinery the $3,300,000,000 Public Works Administration fund has been allocated. By virtue of these expenditures widespread employment is being given.[1]

[1] Mention should undoubtedly be made at this juncture of the newly enacted Housing Act designed, as it is, to further—"prime the pump" by inducing private capital once again to finance the construction of houses. To this end the Federal government proposes to insure loans granted by various financial institutions for the purpose of constructing or renovating houses up to a total of 80 per cent of the loans granted. As it is very improbable that 20 per cent of the loans made will so completely "sour," this is almost the equivalent of a total guarantee. It is hoped thus to reduce the rate of interest charged by the various "finance companies" which varies from 14 to 20 per cent per annum to 7 per cent. And in so doing to stimulate a spirit of building activity which will help start the heavy industries moving again. The liability which the National Housing Administration may assume is limited to $200,000,000.

Mention should also be made of the fact that at the second session of the 73rd Congress, $522,000,000 was appropriated for road building purposes. Most of this fund is to be spent in 1935, although some of the expenditures will undoubtedly carry over to 1936.

CHAPTER THIRTY-TWO

THE PROS AND CONS OF THE PUBLIC WORKS PROGRAM

THE economic theories underlying the expenditure of $3,300,000,000 on a public works program are interesting indeed.

Four variations in reasoning are to be found. The first might be called the balance-wheel theory; the second, the downward-spiral theory; the third, the pump-priming theory; and the fourth, the experimental theory.

Proponents of what is termed the balance-wheel theory survey the economic situation from the point of view of purchasing power. As they see it, the fundamental problem is the maintenance of a steady demand. The function of a program of public works, consequently, is the balancing of any decrease in private employment by an increase in public employment. Thus, in periods of great economic activity, public projects should be curtailed and public works employes returned to their former places in private industry; in periods of depression, the reverse policy should be pursued. They believe that in the present crisis public works should be radically expanded at once, and those now unemployed should be given work thereby. In this fashion, a steady flow of purchasing power might be maintained. The business cycle would not thereby be eliminated, but its fluctuations would be rendered less severe.

Proponents of the downward-spiral theory, although more or less in sympathy with the viewpoint just advanced, analyze the economic situation from a different angle. As they see it, once a depression has started, the forces of liquidation carry us deeper and deeper into the mire, unless or until some counteracting force intervenes. As a depression progresses, one or another of our important economic segments is forced to contract its activities (as in the case of American agriculture, this may be partially due to international competition). Any such contraction of business activity necessarily reduces employment and thus diminishes the total national purchasing power unless some other industry, in the process of expansion, happens to absorb the unemployed. Because of this reduction of purchasing power, other producers sell less and must therefore reduce their payrolls.

Thus the depression gathers momentum. In due time, falling prices, resulting from increased competition for what business there is, undermine the entire price structure. Banks and mortgage-holders take alarm and try to save themselves by forcing payments of both short- and long-term debts. Homes and farms are thrown on the market, the price level is still further depressed. Bank failures follow, and a total collapse of our entire financial structure becomes imminent. This, briefly, is the story of the depression from 1929 to 1933.

In times past, proponents of this theory maintain, certain counteracting forces—railroad building, the discovery of oil fields, automobile manufacture, and the rise of the radio industry—intervened. Presenting the investor with an opportunity to make unusual profits, these developments tapped reservoirs of capital which have not been touched during the present depression, and, in so doing, created additional purchasing power, which halted previous downward spirals and started the wheels of industry turning. The money from those reservoirs of capital was first expended for the construction of new plants and the development of new products; soon finding its way into the pay envelopes of the workers, it was spent for consumption goods, and the forces of recovery got under way. In the history of the latest depression, however, no such development has appeared. Consequently, unless the downward movement is to be allowed to run its course, some counter-deflationary force must be artificially created.

The proponents of the pump-priming theory view the economic picture from still another angle. They assume that the depression was the product of certain maladjustments in our economic order; that a certain amount of liquidation is necessary to bring the various segments of our economy into realignment. They assume that the depression should be and has been allowed to run its course until the necessary liquidation is complete. The only trouble, as they see it, is that the process of deflation has left both finance and business prostrate. There is enough purchasing power left to support the present volume of business, but not enough to cause it to move upward. Unlike the proponents of the downward-spiral theory, they do not believe that the downward spiral will continue until economic life comes to a total standstill, but they agree that some new force must manifest itself before business will recover. This additional force may be a new invention or the radical transformation of an old industry which will attract investment funds. If, however, no such inventions or improvements are in sight—and in the opinion of the proponents of this theory none are—a program of public works is the only alternative.

A fourth variation in the line of reasoning which supports a huge program of public works might be entitled the experimental theory. The exponents of this point of view agree with the adherents of the pump-priming theory that the depression was, in its initial stages, the result of certain maladjustments in our economic life. They believe that these maladjustments can be corrected only by a certain degree of liquidation. They agree with the exponents of the downward-spiral theory that after a depression has started, the forces of deflation are self-generating, and that, in consequence, the sweep of a depression frequently goes much farther than is necessary. Whether the deflationary forces would exhaust themselves, they do not pretend to know. Whether the natural play of economic forces would, if permitted, produce a natural upturn, they admit, is beyond their prophetic vision.

Of one thing, however, they are certain: The onward rush of the deflationary forces from October, 1929, to March 4, 1933, showed no signs of abating. Approximately 9.5 per cent of the farms of the country had already gone under the hammer. An equal number of urban homes, in all probability, had met a similar fate. In their opinion, the lower middle class was rapidly becoming proletarianized. Thirteen million people were out of work. The stage was set for a social disturbance which might shake our social order to its foundations.

They were inclined to doubt the dire predictions of the downward-spiral theorists that the final result of the downward spiral would be the total cessation of all business activity. They were even dubious of the assertion that business was on such a dead center that it could never get off of its own volition. They believed that, in the course of time, this depression would work itself out as have all other depressions in the past. But, how much more would the American people endure? How much more should they be required to endure? Although not agreeing entirely with either of the two preceding schools of thought, the adherents of this fourth theory found themselves in complete accord with them in their analysis of the natural course of a natural recovery. The possibility of artificially creating a counter-deflationary force did not, in consequence, appear to them altogether unfeasible. Could not a tremendous program of public works be fashioned which would tap the reservoirs of capital throughout the country in a fashion similar to that which occurs when railroad bonds are sold to the investing public? Would not such a program, moreover, have exactly the same counter-deflationary effect as the more natural counter-deflationary forces? Needless to say, there is no agreement among economists on the matter.

The critics of a public works program present four major indictments of its validity. First, they assert that a program of this character diverts from the money market funds which might otherwise go into private industry. It seems obvious to them that if the government, through the sale of bonds, extracts $3,300,000,000 from the money market, there is just that much less money seeking investment in private enterprise. Private enterprise, so these critics argue, is in consequence slowed up by just that amount.

The proponents of a program of public works reply to this criticism in two ways. The criticism, so they assert, "rests upon the fallacious assumption of a rigidly limited and inflexible volume of credit." In the second place, during a depression private capital simply piles up in the banks. Investors are too timid to take the ordinary risks of private investment. Safety rather than profit during these abnormal periods is the one and only prerequisite of investment. Hence far from diverting funds from private industry, the government is merely putting to work what would otherwise be inactive capital.

The critics of a program of public works maintain also that many of the public works projected and under construction—low-cost housing, for example—will actually undermine existing values and in so doing may well again start the downward swing. Moreover, in so far as the public works program has maintained wage levels at a higher rate than would otherwise prevail, it has further slowed up private activity. Specifically, the requirement that skilled labor be paid from one dollar to one dollar and twenty cents an hour on public works projects in regions in which wages for even skilled labor had fallen to three dollars or four dollars a day has automatically shut off a considerable portion of the demand for increased construction work which might have developed at the lower wage rate.

The proponents of the public works program for the most part concede the force of these arguments. The question is merely whether or not the greater degree of business activity made possible by the public works program does not much more than offset the business activities thus lost, and whether the increased purchasing power made possible through the maintenance of high wage scales may not very easily constitute the "additional demand" necessary to start the forces of recovery.

The third argument advanced by the critics of a public works program is the tremendous burden of debt which is of necessity accumulated. Sooner or later this burden will have to be paid off. Taxes will have to be doubled or trebled. To the proponents of a program of public works this criticism appears so fallacious as hardly to merit answer. Confident that a program of public works will give the necessary stimulus to American recovery, they insist that the added tax burden will be inconsequential. If by virtue of the stimulus given to recovery by a program of public works costing $3,300,000,000 or even $5,000,000,000, the nation's annual income can be increased from $43,000,000,000 a year to $80,000,000,000 it seems self-evident that the expenditure is justified.

The heart of the criticism of a program of public works, however, is in the assertion that it is not possible to create artificially an anti-deflationary force similar in character to such natural counter-deflationary forces as the development of the automobile, the perfection of the radio, etc., that, in fact, a tremendous difference exists between a public works program and a natural development of this character—which in and of itself renders all reasoning of this character fallacious.

The simplest way to present this criticism is to point out that most economic activities are part of an endless chain. A manufacturer—produces $2,000,000 worth of goods a month. He sells these goods. With the $2,000,000 he purchases—say, for simplicity, $1,000,000 worth of raw materials and $1,000,000 worth of labor. He again sells the goods. He again purchases raw materials and again pays the expenses of labor. Thus the endless chain goes on. Of quite a different character is an outlay of money for public works. The money is spent. There is a temporary expansion of business activity. But no endless chain of economic activity is set up. As a result, slowly but surely, business activity may be expected to recede. The total consequence will be a number of public improvements, and an increase in the public debt. Nothing permanent will have been accomplished.

This argument, as the proponents of a program of public works see it, overlooks three things. In the first place it ignores all questions of psychology. A spurt in business activity extended over a period of twelve or eighteen months may very well generate confidence, which in and of itself is important, for it can probably be stated quite truthfully that an unreasonable lack of confidence is frequently as responsible for the severity of a depression as is overconfidence for the excesses of a boom. The mere restoration of confidence may itself release sufficient purchasing power both of consumption and construction goods as to turn the tide of the depression.

In the second place, in the minds of the proponents of such a plan, public works are in many cases self-generating, not in the sense that they establish an endless chain of economic processes, but in the sense that they indirectly stimulate very far-reaching developments. It seems reasonably clear that our extensive system of hard-surfaced roads had something to do with the development and widespread use of the modern automobile. Similarly, it seems within the realm of reason that the development of a number of tremendous water-power projects which make possible the sale of electricity at two cents per kilowatt, instead of seven cents, may stimulate a hitherto unheard-of development in the electrical equipment and accessories industries. Whether the present program of public works has been consciously fashioned to stimulate coordinate economic activity of this character only a more detailed study of the Public Works Administration than is yet possible would reveal.

Which of these theories relative to public works is sound only time will tell.

CONCLUSION

CHAPTER THIRTY-THREE

SUMMARY AND CONCLUSION

Avowedly experimental in its character, the New Deal was formulated for the threefold purpose of halting the deflation, preventing the proletarianization of the middle class and introducing a better balance into our national economy.

To the end that the self-generative aspects of the depression might be eliminated from our economic life the Emergency Banking Act was passed, designed not only to meet the exigencies of the banking crisis, but also to obviate the necessity for dumping securities on the securities' markets. Thus it was hoped to relieve the securities' market from the necessity of absorbing a volume of selling which would have depressed securities' prices to a point as artificial in its character as the speculative prices of the Coolidge inflation. With this end in view the borrowing power of the Reconstruction Finance Corporation was enlarged. Loans were made to insurance companies, railroads, building-and-loan associations, and various and sundry financial institutions. The objective of these loans was not, needless to say, the welfare of the stockholders of these institutions. Their purpose was rather the prevention of a major failure among these economic units, the failure of any one of which might have, so it was reasoned, such disastrous repercussions throughout our entire economic order as to undermine completely the existing price structure and thus prolong the depression.

Of a similar character was the Home-Owners Loan Act. Home-owner after home-owner was losing his home. House after house was being sold at auction. Urban real estate values were spiraling downward at a terrific pace, undermining still further equities as they went down. The consequence was inevitable. Banks, insurance companies, building-and-loan associations, and other mortgage-lending institutions refused to renew mortgages at the old values. Unable to make the adjustments demanded by these institutions, additional home-owner after home-owner was forced to let his house go under the hammer. Realty prices declined still farther. Thus the self-generating forces of the depression swept on.

To relieve this situation the Home-Owners Loan Act was passed. Two billion two hundred million (now three billion two hundred million) dollars were made available to save the distressed home-owner and, equally important, to relieve the pressure on urban real estate.

Farm after farm was going under the hammer. Foreclosure was following foreclosure. The self-generative forces of the depression were operating in the agricultural regions of the United States with a ruthlessness quite equal to their operation in the cities. The price of rural real estate was dropping precipitously. The Federal Farm Loan Act was passed. Two billion two hundred million dollars were made available to aid the farmer threatened with foreclosure and, equally important, to relieve the pressure upon rural real estate values.

All these measures were designed merely to peg the price level where it stood. They constituted the first line of attack upon the forces of the depression.

The Agricultural Adjustment Act was passed; the agricultural program formulated. Agricultural production was to be curtailed and agricultural prices forced upward. Temporarily at least, subsidies were to be paid those sections of the farming community which had been most drastically affected by the deflationary forces. Similarly, the National Industrial Recovery Act was passed. One of its objectives was the diversion of a larger portion of the national income to labor, whose increased demand should likewise contribute to a rise in prices. The Banking Act of 1934 was also passed. It was intended further to expedite the opening of closed banks, and through a deposit guarantee to entice money back from hiding. In this fashion a second line of attack upon the forces of the depression was formulated, designed not only to peg prices but to advance them.

The remaining measures—the inflationary amendments to the Agricultural Adjustment Act, the various and sundry relief Acts, and the public works program—were of a different character. Through them the real drive on the price level was to be made.

Thus a program designed to halt the deflation was constructed. In the administration thereof mistakes have undoubtedly been made. New problems have been created. Nevertheless, the fact remains that the forces of deflation have, temporarily at least, been held in check. A price rise of no small magnitude has been attained.

Inextricably intertwined with those aspects of the New Deal designed to halt the course of the depression were those intended to prevent the proletarianization of large sections of the middle class.

As a result of the agricultural depression, which started in the United States nine years before the collapse of 1929, some half million farmers had already lost their homes. The percentage of farm tenants had risen from approximately 33 per cent in 1910 to some 50 per cent, so it is estimated, by 1932. The inevitable consequence of the collapse of 1929 was the further accentuation of those forces which had been in operation throughout the decade. How far this transformation of the American farmer into a landless rural proletariat might have proceeded, had governmental action not been taken, it is impossible to estimate. Suffice it to say that fully 40 per cent of the farm acreage of the United States was, in 1929, subject to mortgage.

Only less important, consequently, than the checking of the depression itself was the prevention of the further proletarianization of the American farmer. With this end in view the administration's agricultural program was formulated. Whether as a result of this program or not, the fact is that since the inauguration of the program, foreclosures of farm properties have diminished radically. Farm prices have risen moderately. Temporarily at least the proletarianization of this section of the American middle class has been checked.

Hardly any less serious than the proletarianization of the American farmer which had been one of the consequences of the depression was the equally rapid proletarianization of the urban home-owner. The number of home-owners who were forced to lose the properties in which they had invested their life savings has never been tabulated. A conservative estimate would certainly place the figure well above a half million. Hundreds of thousands more were hanging on only by the narrowest equities. Unless the administration was willing to see the transformation of America from a home-owning people to one held by no fixed ties of property, action was imperative. The home-owners' relief program was formulated.

Whether as a result of this program or not, the number of foreclosures has been drastically reduced. Temporarily, at least, the proletarianization of another large section of the American middle class has been prevented.

Equally acute in many cases was the position of the savings banks and insurance companies in which another large section of the middle class had deposited their life savings. Once again the administration was confronted with the question as to whether it was better to stand by while this section of the middle class was rendered propertyless or whether governmental action was imperative. To the end that these institutions might be saved increased appropriations to the Reconstruction Finance Corporation were authorized and a drive on the price level begun. As a consequence of these policies another large section of the middle class has temporarily at least been saved from the poverty which was inevitable had the forces of the depression swept on.

Equally dire, needless to say, was the condition of the unemployed. To alleviate their condition the Federal Emergency Relief Act was passed, the Civilian Conservation Corps created, the Civil Works Administration established, and the Public Works program inaugurated. The relief of the unemployed, however, can hardly be considered one of the cardinal objectives of the New Deal. Temporary relief would have been extended whatever administration was in office, whatever recovery program had been adopted. In the long run, however, the success or failure of the New Deal will be measured by the degree to which unemployment relief becomes once again an incidental problem of our social organization.

Part and parcel of the attempts to halt the deflation and the efforts to prevent the further proletarianization of the middle class has been the endeavor to introduce a better balance into our national economy. To this end the agricultural program was formulated, designed, as we have already indicated, to increase the income of the agrarian section of the community. With this end in view certain of the maladjustments in the field of finance have been corrected. The National Industrial Recovery Act has been passed. A Federal Coordinator of Railroads has been established. And the other constituent parts of the New Deal have been inaugurated.

How effective these attempts to introduce a balanced economy into the United States will prove remains to be seen.

One thing only is certain. At the moment the United States is much better off by virtue of the recovery program than it was before that program was inaugurated.

What the future holds—whether the new problems which have been created as a result of the New Deal will more than offset the gains which have been made—only time can tell.

INDEX

INDEX

New Deal

500

MAY 6 - '35
MAY 28 '58
DEC 20
MAY 4